To Amanda
To Cynthia
and
To the Memory of Aldous Huxley

The Centering Book

AWARENESS ACTIVITIES FOR CHILDREN AND ADULTS TO RELAX THE BODY AND MIND

GAY HENDRICKS

and

RUSSEL WILLS

PRENTICE HALL PRESS
NEW YORK   LONDON   TORONTO   SYDNEY   TOKYO

Prentice Hall Press
Gulf + Western Building
One Gulf + Western Plaza
New York, New York 10023

PRENTICE HALL PRESS and colophon are registered trademarks of Simon & Schuster Inc.

Library of Congress Cataloging-in-Publication Data

Hendricks, Gay.
  The centering book : awareness activities for children and adults
to relax the body and mind / Gay Hendricks and Russel Wills.
    p.   cm.
  Bibliography: p.
  ISBN 0-13-122276-7
  1. Affective education. 2. Self-actualization (Psychology)
3. Movement education. I. Wills, Russel. II. Title.
[LB1072.H46   1989]
371.3'07'8—dc19   89-3544
                                                                       CIP

Text illustrated by Nancy Hendrick

Manufactured in the United States of America

10 9 8 7 6 5 4 3 2 1

Contents

Preface

TRANSPERSONAL EDUCATION:
DEVELOPING THE WHOLE PERSON

There is a feeling of balance, a feeling of inner strength that we feel when we are *centered*. To feel centered is to experience one's psychological center of gravity—a solid integration of mind and body. The authors believe that knowing how to feel centered is as important to young people as knowing how to read, write, and brush teeth.

This book contains activities that people use to help themselves feel centered; all of the techniques can be used in the classroom and in the home, and they can be used by people of all ages. The authors' goal is to make centering techniques available to everyone.

Schools place a great deal of emphasis on the development of cognitive, rational, and intellectual processes. To balance this emphasis, *The Centering Book* provides the core of a curriculum for the development of affective, intuitive, and creative processes in students. Both types of development are important: in fact, the full development of one may depend on the concurrent development of the other. Furthermore, many parents want to help their children develop their maximum potential, and, therefore, this book can also be used in the home to provide a set of activities that parents and children can use to explore new levels of awareness together.

The sources of the activities include yoga, Zen, movement, imagery, relaxation training, the Senoi people of the Central Malay Peninsula, and the Sufi tradition. Children enjoy these activities because they find them interesting, useful, and relaxing. Adults enjoy them because exploring new spaces with children is an enlightening experience.

Welcome to our book.

The
Centering Book

Introduction

Most of us agree that education needs new directions. There are comprehensive statements of educational problems in books such as Silberman's *Crisis in the Classroom*, and there are moving personal statements in books by Jonathan Kozol, John Holt, George Dennison, James Herndon, and others. Books such as these have increased our awareness that schools are in drastic need of change. In addition, many of us have had personal experiences that convinced us even more that school is a joyless experience for many students and teachers.

Take a moment to recall your own schooling. Compare your memories with what you know about schools today. The buildings are prettier now, but are there many substantial differences in the type of education our children are receiving? If your answer is yes, you are fortunate to be where you are. If it is no, you are in the majority. Most of us agree that our education could have taught us more things we needed to know. We learned a lot of facts, but didn't we really want to know how to live and be happy?

We need to ask ourselves what schools are for.

Should they help people live their lives, or should they assume that life skills are best learned outside of school? Should our schools teach relevant skills, or should they be content to teach only moderately useful material such as arithmetic and geography? Questions such as these are important because millions of people are affected by the answers.

Focusing on deficits sometimes puts us into negative states, so we have filled this book with solutions instead of problems. However, a few facts about education should be mentioned because they are so obvious that they are frequently taken for granted.

LIMITED SKILLS

Schools teach a very limited set of skills. Reading and mathematics are useful, but only to a point. Skills such as these are not very important when measured against the other things we do with our lives. Reading and mathematics, however, are two of the *most* useful skills currently taught in our schools. In contrast, much of the other material children learn in school is virtually useless. A teacher we know gave us a good example of useless material. He remembers the experience of slavishly memorizing the states and their natural resources when he was in the sixth grade. In particular, he remembers learning that Alaska's natural resources were seal fur and whale blubber. He did well on the test, which was a good short-term achievement, but no one ever asked him these facts again, so that was the only chance he had to use them. A few years later, though, something important happened: gold and oil were discovered in Alaska, replacing fur and blubber as the major natural resources. He had learned a set of facts that were useless until they became obsolete.

It is a trite observation that schools are obsessed with facts, but this condition still exists. We do children a disservice if we lead them to believe that facts are what is important in life.

EMPHASIS ON COGNITIVE SKILLS

In general, schools are concerned only with the intellectual development of children. Although lip service is paid to affective or social-emotional objectives, little is being done to achieve them. This cognitive emphasis is tragic, for it represents, at best, only half of the human mind. Processes such as feeling, fantasy, interaction, and intuition are as important as intellectual processes Such social-emotional processes as these underlie and enhance the development of cognitive processes. Ignoring one type of process causes the other to remain hobbled.

There is a field of research that is investigating the functions of the two hemispheres of the brain. It appears that speech and linear thought are processes that belong primarily to one hemisphere of the brain (usually the left). The other half of the brain appears to direct the more "mystical" functions such as visual-spatial thinking, intuition, and creativity. If this research continues in its likely direction, it may become clear that our schools are allowing half of the human brain to lie virtually fallow.

WHAT CAN BE DONE?

There are many things to be done, but this is not the place to discuss all of the political, economic, psychological, and social changes that would be needed to overhaul our schools. There are, however, several specific suggestions that we can make.

Schools should emphasize processes instead of facts. For example, instead of having children memorize the natural resources of the states, we could spend the same amount of time teaching them the process of memorization. By learning a process, children could then insert any sort of content into their memories, from chemical formulas to telephone numbers. There are many excellent techniques available for increasing memory skills. Obviously, there are many processes more important than memory skills (decision making and changing one's own behavior, to name two), and we should be making every effort to teach important cognitive and social-emotional processes to children.

Schools should teach meaningful skills. One way you can determine if a skill is meaningful is to determine the number of bad things that can happen to you if you do not have a skill. Another way is to determine the amount of joy a skill can bring. For example, how many unpleasant things can happen to you if you cannot recall geography facts? Compare the ability to recall geography with the ability to communicate feelings congruently. Most unpleasant situations can be averted through the honest expression of feeling; in addition, our moments of greatest joy come when we share our deepest positive feelings and thereby extend them into other people.

One of the most meaningful skills is the process of psychological integration that we call centering. Centering helps people develop a pool of inner stillness that facilitates appropriate action. To be centered is to have the intellect and the intuition working in harmony. As we begin to integrate our bodies and minds, we feel balanced and more responsive to our environment. Schools should help people become more responsive to their environment.

IN SUMMARY

We believe that transpersonal education is the answer to many of our educational problems. Transpersonal education draws upon previous educational psychologies, such as psychoanalytic, behavioral, and humanistic approaches, but goes beyond them to seek a synthesis in education of intellect and intuition, mind and body, fact and feeling. We believe such a synthesis should be the ultimate aim of education.

We have talked about some of the things that are wrong with schools, and some of the things that could be done to improve them. We have talked about some of the good things that can happen when people begin to feel centered. Now we invite you to turn the page and experience firsthand the process of centering.

On Reading
Instructions

The descriptions of most of the activities begin with a few explanatory sentences. Suggestions for organizing the group are also included. The material that follows the heading "INSTRUCTIONS" is designed to be communicated directly to the group. Rather than reading the directions verbatim, we hope you will ad-lib them so that the instructions will come from you instead of from the book.

It helps to give the instructions in a peaceful, soothing tone of voice. The best way for you to get in touch with this tone of voice is to tell yourself to relax, and to listen to the tone of voice you use on yourself. When you find a way of speaking that sounds harmonious to you, use it with the children.

Some of the instructions are written in a flowing, almost hypnotic style that may at first look odd on the printed page. Try reading these instructions orally, and you will probably get a feeling for the reason they were written in that style.

I

Basic Centering

The Experience of Centering

Most teachers and parents wish to help young people develop as whole persons, which means that a balance must be attained among cognitive, social, and emotional potentials. Centering helps young people achieve this balance while giving them a set of skills they can use to feel emotionally strong and solid. Of course, many teachers use centering techniques to help children develop cognitive processes; for example, centering is ideal for helping children calm down before a test. But centering techniques are also useful as self-concept creators. Young people who know how to center themselves have skills they can use for the rest of their lives.

Centering is one of those things you must experience in order to understand. Five children described the feeling in five different, but related ways:

Being lined up just right.
Feeling solid.
Not thinking—just feeling.
Being right on.
Being balanced.

Although each person's experience of centering is a little different, all the people we have encountered like the feeling.

Feeling the Center

This activity is best done on the floor, the children either sitting cross-legged or lying on their backs. If the sitting position is used, remind the group members to sit squarely on their sitting bones, with spines straight and hands relaxed in lap. If the lying position is used, be sure everyone is lying straight—legs relaxed and loose, back and head in straight alignment.

INSTRUCTIONS

"Most of the time we use only a small part of our lungs when we breathe. If we can learn to fill our bodies with breath by breathing more deeply and smoothly, we can increase the energy that flows through our bodies. Let's begin by letting our bodies relax . . . becoming very comfortable and closing our eyes.

"And now, becoming aware of your feet and moving them around a little to become aware of how they feel, send them a message to relax. Let all of the tension go out of them and feel them rest comfortably on the floor.

"Now relax your legs. Let go of them and let them sink into the floor, feeling relaxed and heavy.

"Let the feeling of relaxation enter your chest and your stomach. Feel the middle of your body become soothed and relaxed. Breathe deeply and smoothly, letting all of the tension go out of your body.

"Now let your neck and face relax. Feel the tension draining out of your face as you feel the soothing feeling of relaxation enter your face and your neck.

"Relax your arms and your hands, feeling them resting comfortably, completely supported. Breathe deeply, sending the feeling of relaxation to your arms and hands."

Pause (thirty seconds)

"Inhale slowly through your nose. Let your stomach fill up with breath, then fill your chest. Breathe out smoothly, emptying your chest first, then your stomach. Try to let the breath come and go smoothly and peacefully. Let it flow in and out of your body, filling your body with energy. Feel yourself breathing deeply and smoothly, the energy flowing in and out of you. Listen to your breath flowing in and out of you."

Pause (ten breaths)

"The center of your body is where it balances. For many people the balance point is just below the navel. As you breathe in, imagine that your breath is pouring into your body through the center of your body. Let yourself feel the energy rushing into your body through the center, just below the navel. Feel your breath flow into your body, up through your chest, filling your head. Hold the breath inside you for a moment, then let it flow out, carrying with it any tension you feel. Breathe through your center, filling your body with energy, then let the breath flow out of you, relaxing your body completely."

Pause (ten breaths)

"Let yourself feel the center of your body, so that you can come back to it when you want to relax and feel balanced. Anytime you have something in your head that you don't like, breathe it out and then replace it with pure, clean energy when you breathe in.

"Now feel the alertness coming into your body. Feel your feet and hands begin to stir. Feel your muscles begin to move. Open your eyes, feeling rested and full of energy."

Ear Centering

This activity will put you and the kids in touch with a peaceful sound you may never have noticed before. Ear centering can be done sitting or lying down.

INSTRUCTIONS

"Most of the time, our ears do not hear much of what is going on around us in the world. Now, though, let's relax and see how many sounds we can pick up.

"Close your eyes and let your body feel peaceful and

relaxed. Take a few deep breaths, and feel all of the tension drain out of your body. Let yourself go completely, feeling the soothing sense of relaxation fill your body.

"Relax and become aware of your ears."

Pause (ten seconds)

"Let your ears pick up all the sounds you can hear outside the room."

Pause (two minutes)

"Now let your ears pick up all the sounds you can hear inside the room."

Pause (two minutes)

"Now be very silent and listen to the sound inside your ears. Listen to this sound and let it fill your head."

Pause

"Now listen to that sound with the center of your body instead of with your ears."

Pause

"You can return to that sound when you want to feel relaxed and peaceful. When you want to feel more calm just relax your body and listen to your inner sound. It is a soothing sound that will help you learn to listen to your body.

"Now it is time to let your awareness come back to the room. Feel the alertness coming slowly into your hands, your feet, your chest, your head, moving slowly. You are feeling rested and alert."

COMMENT

On a good day everybody hears inner sounds; on a not-so-good day some do and some don't. Explain to the children that this depends on how quiet we are, and invite them to listen for the sounds on their own.

Eye Centering

We use our eyes all the time, and most of us rarely stop to rest them. Here is an activity that teaches centering while allowing the eyes some relaxation.

Have everyone sit in a cross-legged position, with spines straight. Everyone should face in the same direction.

INSTRUCTIONS

"This is an exercise to help our eyes feel stronger and more rested. Take a few breaths to relax your bodies. Let all of your attention go to your eyes."

Pause

"Move your eyes slowly up and down as far as they will go. Do this five times, then rest them in the center."

Pause

"Move your eyes slowly from side to side as far as they will go. Do this five times, then rest them in the center."

Pause

"Move your eyes from top left to bottom right five times, then rest them in the center." *(Pointing may help.)*

Pause

"Move your eyes from top right to bottom left five times, then rest them in the center."

Pause

"Move your eyes clockwise in a circle five times then rest them in the center."

Pause

"Move your eyes counterclockwise in a circle five times, then rest them in the center."

Pause

"Now imagine that you are seeing through the center of your body rather than just through your eyes."

Pause

"Now rub your hands together until they are warm. Close your eyes and cup your hands over them, letting them absorb the warmth. Open your eyes in the darkness and let them enjoy the warmth (ten to thirty seconds).

Now close your eyes and uncup your hands. And now open your eyes slowly and let the light come in."

Sinking to the Center

This is a peaceful but powerful breathing technique that gives children a feeling of quiet control. Start with two or three minutes of it, then work up to more.

The proper position for this activity is kneeling, sitting lightly on the heels with the spine straight.

INSTRUCTIONS

"Find a good spot where you can sit squarely and where your body feels comfortable. Let the lower part of your spine be straight and let your shoulders be relaxed. Let your muscles relax until your body feels calm and peaceful. Let your eyes close slowly."

Pause

"Begin exhaling slowly and smoothly through your mouth. Make a small sound so that you can hear whether it's smooth or not. When you exhale all your breath, give one final puff to make sure all the air is gone. Now relax and let the air enter your body slowly through your nose."

Pause

"Again exhale smoothly through your mouth. Let the breath come out slowly but powerfully, as if you are sending your breath to the other end of the universe. When you feel all the air is gone, make one final effort to get it all out."

Pause

"Now begin inhaling through the nose. Draw in the air as if you are sending it out the back of your head. Send it out the back of your head and let your lungs fill up by themselves."

Pause

"When you've inhaled completely, hold your breath for a few seconds, then relax your body and let the breath sink down through your body to your center, just below your navel."

Pause

"When you feel your breath in your center, hold it a moment, then begin to exhale smoothly, slowly, powerfully through your mouth. Send the breath all the way to the other end of the universe."

Pause

(Repeat the key instructions several times until everyone understands the important images.)

WHEN READY TO FINISH

"Now return slowly to breathing your usual way. Let your body feel calm, still, centered."

Pause (twenty seconds)

"Now open your eyes slowly and let the sight of the room in. Rise slowly to your feet, feeling relaxed and refreshed."

COMMENT

If any of the children feel lightheaded, tell them to breathe normally for a few moments.

Energy Rising

People seldom understand this exercise when they read it to themselves, because their brains are too busy reading to experience the images. We recommend saving it until you can have someone read it to you.

This activity comes from Tibet, by way of our friend Jack Downing. It is a way of uniting center, chest, and head. The best position for energy rising is sitting cross-legged in a circle, with spines straight.

INSTRUCTIONS

"Let's close our eyes and let our bodies relax. Shift around a little until you find a spot where your body rests comfortably. Let a few soothing breaths flow into your body and let yourself go."

Pause (thirty seconds)

"Now feel a little spot of energy at the bottom of your stomach, in the center of your body. You may imagine it as a light, or a warm spot, or just a spot of energy. Relax your body and feel the spot of energy in the center of your body, deep within you."

Pause (fifteen seconds)

"Breathe in slowly through your nose, and as you do, let each breath make your spot of energy larger. Breathing in on it makes the spot grow. Relax, and breathe smoothly, letting each breath make the spot a little larger. Let it expand to fill your stomach, breathing slowly and deeply."

Pause (one minute)

"Now your stomach is filled, and you may continue breathing on your stomachful of energy as it slowly expands upward to fill your chest."

Pause (one minute)

"Now feel your stomach and chest filled with

energy, and as you breathe, feel your energy expand. Now let the energy flow up through your neck into your head. Breathe slowly, and feel each breath expanding the energy up into your head."

Pause (one minute)

"Let the energy circulate freely from the bottom of your stomach, up through your chest, up to the top of your head. Relax, and feel the energy flow throughout your body, and as you do, feel those parts of your body as one. Feel the flow of energy circulate through your body."

Pause (one minute)

"Now it's time to become alert again. Let's begin to move our fingers and toes a little. Let your legs feel lively and full of energy. Let your eyes open slowly. When your eyes are fully open, stand up, feeling refreshed and relaxed."

The Quick Centering Breath

Once we learn how to contact the center, we can use it to relax, to pull ourselves together when we feel scattered, and to feel better, even when we aren't feeling bad. This activity can be done in any position.

INSTRUCTIONS

"Focus all of your attention on your center. Send all of your thoughts and feelings down to that point just below your navel."

Pause (ten seconds)

"Now begin sending each breath all the way down to your center."

Pause (ten seconds)

"Each time you breathe, send the breath to your center."

Pause (ten seconds)

"Now that you know how to get in touch with your center, you can focus on that point when you feel nervous or angry, or whenever you want to feel better . . . it's always there when you need it."

Instant Centering

One of the reasons centering feels so good is that it clears our heads of scattered, cluttering thoughts. Here are several quick images to which young people have responded very well.

INSTRUCTIONS

Have the students put all their thoughts in an elevator up in their heads. Then have them punch the button and send the elevator down to their centers.

Have the students imagine an hourglass inside them, the top in their heads, the bottom in their centers. Have them let the sand slowly fill up the bottom.

Have the students imagine a light shining out from their centers, and have them vary the intensity of the light.

Side-Stepping Negative Energy

Young people receive a lot of verbal hostility from parents, teachers, and peers. Hardly a day passes in which someone doesn't tell them to sit down, shut up, eat their beans, go jump in a lake, or not to do that again as long as they live. Often, these demands are made in angry and hurtful ways. One of the interesting things about anger is that it is often misdirected: we get mad at one person or thing and take it out on another.

It helps to regard anger as negative energy. Some types of negative energy are best side-stepped. For example, the negative energy of a bullet is better ducked than confronted. Similarly, the best way to defend against a hostile attack is to step aside and let the attacker fall on his face through his own negative energy. This way is best because it requires us to expend much less energy than we would if we resisted and fought back. If we resist, we are likely to "catch" the force of his negative energy, and we must then do something with this force. Most often, we throw it back in the form of our own negative energy. Then we are responding on the same level as our attacker, which makes it possible that we will be defeated.

After discussing the principles of misdirected anger, you may teach your children any of the following techniques. Role-playing games are helpful in learning how to use these techniques.

THINGS TO DO WHEN PEOPLE SAY BAD THINGS TO YOU

Imagine the bad thing is like a breeze that you can feel go by you.

Imagine the bad thing is like an arrow that sails by as you step aside.

Ask, "Are you sure you're mad at the right person?"

Say, "It hurts when I get yelled at."

Make a circle with your thumb and forefinger.

(for very young children) Imagine you are a duck,

and the bad thing slips off you like water off a duck's back.

COMMENTS

These activities have transformed many homes and classrooms, and it is interesting to consider the reasons for this. First, regarding anger as just another form of energy seems to put it in perspective. Second, all of these activities involve doing something *consciously* in the presence of anger. Most often we react unconsciously when we are attacked, thus playing the same game as our attacker. Giving people a conscious action to perform in the presence of anger can give them that split second that's needed to put the situation in perspective.

2

Relaxing the Mind

Thought Watching

One of the most interesting worlds to explore is the world inside our heads. Something is always going on there, even when we're sleeping.

Although it is essential that we learn to observe our thought processes in our quest for self-understanding, we do not learn as much as we could for at least two reasons. First, it takes practice to learn to observe accurately, and we do not receive much encouragement for engaging in this type of activity. Second, we are too evaluative in our observations. No sooner do we see a thought or feeling than we rush to label it *good* or *bad, right* or *wrong*.

One type of meditation, which originated in the

Orient, involves just watching our thoughts in a non-evaluative way. The goal is to see the thoughts, images, and sounds as they are, without making judgments about them. And when we find ourselves making judgments about the thoughts, we try to observe those judgments. This activity can be done sitting or lying down.

INSTRUCTIONS

"Settle back and let your body relax, and as your body begins to quiet down and become comfortable, let your eyelids close. Relax a while in the darkness, letting your body become peaceful and comfortable. As you lie there, feel around until you find a place where you can find your pulse, and when you do, rest your fingers lightly on that place and get in touch with the quiet rhythm of your pulse as it moves the blood through your body."

Pause (thirty seconds)

"And now in the quiet, let's begin watching our thoughts and feelings that come through our minds . . . just looking and listening for the pictures and sounds in our heads. Pictures, voices, scenes, music, whatever comes in, just watch and listen . . . just observe. When you find yourself lost in thought, just return to watching and listening."

Pause (three to four minutes; work up to about ten minutes as the exercise is repeated).

"Now in the future, when you find yourself angry, sad, or bored, or in any kind of mood, happy or sad, just watch and listen to what is going on inside your head. This will help get you in touch with how you are feeling.

"Let yourself become alert at your own speed. Feel the alertness come into your body, stretching a little to feel more alert. Open your eyes and let the light in, feeling rested and calm."

Counting Breaths

One of the best ways to quiet the mind is to focus on breathing; there is something very relaxing about the smooth ebb and flow of breath. Sitting cross-legged is a good position for this activity.

INSTRUCTIONS

"Find a spot that feels good to sit on, moving your body around until you feel comfortable and light. This is an activity in which we pay attention to our breath. As you become comfortable, begin paying attention to the way the breath comes in and out of your body. And as you listen to your breath, begin counting each breath, each time you breathe in . . . counting to ten, then starting again with one. When your mind wanders, bring it gently back to one and start again."

Pause (one to two minutes at first, then gradually increase this as the exercise is repeated)

"All of our minds wander, and this exercise helps us know when it's happening. As long as you know it's wandering, you can have more control over where it goes. And now watch your attention come right back here as you get up, feeling comfortable and alert."

Walking and Centering

This is a simple movement meditation that can be done indoors and outdoors. It is a good activity for turning down the volume of our mental chatter while becoming more aware of our experience of the world around us.

INSTRUCTIONS

"Much of the time we are not aware of how we move through the world, because we are too busy listening to the chatter in our minds. Today, as we walk we will do something to quiet our minds while we walk, so we can be more aware of how we move and how we make contact with the earth.

"And now let's begin walking along, smoothly and easily, and as we find a pace that feels good, not too fast and not too slow, let's begin to say this sentence in time with our walking. The sentence is 'I listen and I see.' And now let's all begin saying it out loud."

Pause (twenty seconds)

"Now, as we move let's say the sentence quietly to ourselves."

Pause (twenty seconds)

"And now begin saying the sentence in your mind, smoothly and easily. If your mind wanders, simply return to saying 'I listen and I see.'"

(Walk for three to five minutes.)

"And now let's slow down and stop. Let's close our eyes and stand still for a moment . . . feeling calm and peaceful . . . feeling our feet and how they make contact with the earth. And when you're ready, open your eyes, letting a feeling of rested alertness fill your bodies."

3

Expanding
Perception

The Art of Seeing

Most of us know how to *look*, but we do not use our ability to *see*. One way to see is to look at something until the mind quits trying to organize it in the same old way.

A blue vase or a candle are good objects to look at. We use a candle in the activity below. Organize the group in a circle around the candle.

INSTRUCTIONS

"Sit down and let your body become comfortable. Move around until you are sitting squarely . . . balanced . . . calm. Take a couple of deep breaths, letting all of the tension flow out of your body."

Pause (ten seconds)

"Now let's begin to watch the candle's flame . . . relaxing our bodies and looking at the candle . . . feeling our eyes relax and accept the image of the flame. Just relax and let the candle have all of your attention . . . and if your mind wanders, just let it return to watching the candle."

(Five to ten minutes is good for this, though you should not stop until the children are ready to.)

"Now close your eyes and watch the images inside your eyes."

Pause (one minute)

"Now open your eyes slowly . . . seeing the brightness of the room . . . feeling rested and alert. Stretch your arms and legs and stand up, feeling rested and peaceful."

Sensing Holes in the World

Take a walk with the children on a sunny day. Cue them that it will be a special kind of walk in which you will help them tune in to a part of the world they usually miss.

INSTRUCTIONS

"As you walk, pay attention to your body . . . how it feels . . . the swing of your arms and the movement of your legs. Let your body relax and swing free, moving easily along the ground. Feel the contact with the earth, and as you move along, begin to watch the shadows of things rather than the things themselves. Relax your eyes and focus them softly. Instead of seeing the leaves of the tree, see the shadows of the leaves. Pretend that you are a shadow, and that you must watch the shadows of things to get around in the world."

(Walk for five to ten minutes.)

"Now let's use our ears for a while, and as we walk, let's listen to the spaces between sounds rather than the sounds themselves. Listen for the quiet holes between sounds . . . the spaces between the things we hear."

Pause (five minutes)

"And now let's stand quietly for a moment, soaking up all of the sights and sounds around us in the world."

Sensing Energy in the World

This is another walk that tunes up the senses. It is best done on a day when the wind is stirring.

INSTRUCTIONS

"Let's begin walking slowly over the ground, keeping our bodies loose and free, relaxing as we move."

(Walk for twenty to thirty seconds.)

"Now begin to notice the little ups and downs in the ground as you move over it. Feel the way the earth rises and falls."

(Walk for twenty to thirty seconds.)

"Now begin feeling the energy of the wind on your skin. Is it with you or against you? Are you moving through it or is it pushing you from in front or behind?"

(Walk for twenty to thirty seconds.)

"Now feel the energy of the wind connecting with the center of your body."

(Walk until it feels right to stop.)

4

Relaxing the Body

Deep Relaxation

Relaxation is one of the most important skills we can learn; it has many uses in education and in the family. Teachers use relaxation to help children improve test scores, sports performance, and social skills. Parents use it to quiet restless bodies at bedtime. No matter what the activity, a relaxed body seems to help.

This activity, done lying on the floor, helps quiet the body by dissolving muscle tension. Although this is a long exercise, children can, with practice, reach the state of relaxation instantly.

For this and later activities, it is nice to have mats or a rug on the floor.

INSTRUCTIONS

"This is an activity that can help us learn to relax our bodies and minds by tensing and releasing muscles. We cannot be tense and relaxed at the same time, so if we learn to relax we can avoid wasting energy through muscle tension. If you ever feel tense, while asking a question or taking a test or anytime, you can use the feeling of relaxation to feel better.

"Let's begin by lying on our backs on the floor and not touching anyone else. Wiggle around a little until you find a way of lying down that is completely comfortable. Now close your eyes and think of your hands. Feel the bones inside them, feel the muscles that move the bones, feel the weight of them on the floor. Now make a fist with your hands and clench tightly. Hold your hands tightly *(ten seconds)*. Now relax and feel the soothing, tingling feeling of relaxation come into your hands."

Pause (ten seconds or so between instructions)

"Now draw up your arms and tighten your biceps as tight as you can. Hold them tightly (ten seconds). Now relax and feel the tension drain out of your arms."

Pause

"Shrug your shoulders now, pushing them as if to

push them up through your ears. Hold them tightly there (ten seconds). Now let them go and feel all the tension drain out of your body."

Pause

"Continuing to keep your eyes closed, open your mouth as far as it will go, stretching the muscles at the corners of your mouth. Hold it tightly (ten seconds). Relax and enjoy the tingling feeling as the tension dissolves in your mouth."

Pause

"Now press your tongue against the roof of your mouth and tighten your jaw muscles. Press tightly and hold it (ten seconds). Now let go and relax. Let the peaceful feeling of relaxation flow through your body."

Pause

"Now wrinkle your nose and make a face. Scrunch up your face tightly and hold it (ten seconds). Relax now, feeling the tension flow out of your face."

Pause

"Now tighten the muscles of your chest, stomach, and abdomen. Draw all of the muscles in tightly and hold them tense (ten seconds). Now let them go, feeling the soothing feeling of relaxation pour in."

Pause

"Now tense the muscles of your thighs by straightening your legs. Hold them tightly (ten seconds). Now relax your thighs—let all of the tension drain out of them."

Pause

"Now tense the backs of your legs by straightening your feet. Hold your legs tensely (ten seconds). Now relax them and let all of the tension go."

Pause

"Now tense your feet by curling the toes. Keep them curled tightly (ten seconds). Now relax your toes and feel the delicious feeling of relaxation come into your feet."

Pause

"Your whole body is feeling loose and relaxed now. Feel yourself completely supported by the floor, and breathe deeply, and as you breathe in, let each breath fill your body with deeper and deeper feelings of relaxation."

Pause

"See if there are any places of tension left in your body. If you feel tense in some area, take a deep breath and send the breath to that place. Fill that tense area with breath, and let the feeling of tension leave your body."

Pause

"Let the soothing feeling of relaxation fill your body. Each breath takes you deeper and deeper into relaxation."

Pause (thirty seconds to one minute)

"Now you will be coming out of relaxation in a moment, and you will feel rested and alert. I will count backward from ten to one, and as I do, feel your body becoming alert at your own rate.

"Ten, nine, eight, feel the alertness returning to your body. Seven, six, five, feel your toes and fingers begin to move. Four, three, move your arms and legs. Two, eyes. One, get up slowly, feeling completely rested and alert."

Instant Relaxation

This relaxation exercise can be done sitting, standing, or lying down. It gives children a skill to counter tension in all kinds of situations. For example, teachers often notice that students squirm while reading aloud, taking tests, or engaging in other anxiety-arousing situations. Older students have these problems, and they also have social situations with which they must contend. In addition to countering tension, instant relaxation can serve as a quick prelude to any of the activities in this book.

INSTRUCTIONS

"Let's close our eyes.

"Now tense every muscle in your body at the same time. Legs, arms, jaws, fists, face, shoulders, stomach. Hold them . . . tightly. Now relax and feel the tension pour out of your body. Let all of the tension flow out of your body and your mind . . . replacing the tension with calm, peaceful energy . . . letting each breath you take bring calmness and relaxation into your body."

Pause

"Now tense your body again and hold it for a few seconds. Then let go, relaxing and feeling all of the tension flow out of your body."

Pause

"And now tense every muscle in your body and at the same time take a deep breath. Hold your body tense and hold your breath for a few seconds. Then say 'relax' to yourself, and when you do, let your breath go and relax."

Pause

"Take a deep breath and hold it about ten seconds. Then say 'relax' to yourself and let yourself go."

Pause

"When you feel like relaxing, just take a deep breath, hold it a few seconds, say 'relax' to yourself, and let it all go. You can do this wherever you are, because nobody can hear you or see you. Practice this again by yourself two or three times."

Pause

"Now let's open our eyes slowly, feeling calm and alert."

Talking to the Body

One of the most important goals of education and child rearing is to help children develop a positive self-image. One of the steps in building a positive self-image is building a positive body image. We *are* our bodies, and it makes no sense to think of the self-image as involving only the head.

This activity is a good way for us to initiate a dialogue with our bodies. It can be done sitting or lying down.

INSTRUCTIONS

"Wander around until you find a spot that feels good, then sit down (lie down) on your spot. Let your body move around until it finds a comfortable place, and then let it settle down on that spot, comfortably supported by the floor. Now we are going to go through various parts of the body, telling each part to relax, and as you tell each part to relax, you will be able to feel a soothing feeling of relaxation enter that part of your body. Now let your attention go to your feet."

Pause (five seconds)

"Tell your feet to relax."

Pause (ten seconds each time)

"Tell your hands to relax."

Pause (ten seconds each time)

"Tell your legs to relax."

Pause (ten seconds each time)

"Tell your arms to relax."

Pause (ten seconds each time)

"Tell your stomach to relax."

Pause

"Tell your shoulders to relax."

Pause

"Tell your chest to relax."

Pause

"Tell your neck to relax."

Pause

"Tell your face to relax."

Pause

"Tell your mind to relax."

Pause

"You can use this feeling of relaxation whenever you want to feel more comfortable and relaxed. Just tell your whole body to relax, and it will listen to you. Now I will count from ten down to one, and as I do, you will feel yourself becoming more alert. Ten, nine, eight, seven, feel your body beginning to stir . . . six, five, four, let your mind wake up . . . three, two, one, sit up, feeling rested and alert."

5

Working with Dreams

Using Dreams in the Classroom

Dreams are one of the major states of consciousness, and we believe they should receive more attention in the developing person. If our goal is to develop an education for the whole person, we cannot afford to neglect dreams.

Dreams can be used educationally in many ways. First, they can be used as material for various projects. An English teacher in San Francisco uses dreams as material for creative writing and drama, and a primary teacher in Connecticut has children use their dreams for art projects in which the children illustrate the stories of their dreams in various media. Second, dreams can be used as tools for self-understanding. In the following section, we have developed a series of activities that employ dreams in the process of personal growth, and that can be used in the classroom and in the home.

Senoi Dream-Work
The People and the Principles[1]

Imagine it is early morning, and you have just been jangled out of the dreamworld by your alarm clock. Your dreams begin to fade as you rush through breakfast, gulp down coffee, and hurry to work. Think how unsettling it is.

Now remember how you feel when you come out of a dream slowly, making a gradual transition to waking, relishing the dream images and incorporating them into your life, sharing your dreams with those with whom you are close. How unusual it is in our society to make communal something as private as a dream.

[1] The authors wish to acknowledge their debt to the work of the late Kilton Stewart, who introduced Senoi dream theory to the outside world, and to the personal communications of our friend Dr. John Sundsten, who lived recently among the Temiar tribe of the Senoi. In assembling this collection of techniques, the authors drew on both of the above sources. The authors have modified the techniques and arranged them in a form that can be used by Westerners in working with their dreams.

Most people do not give much thought to their dreams. If they do realize the importance of dreams at all, they are often justifiably put off by the complicated dream interpretations that fill the traditional psychology literature. Furthermore, our society does not have institutions that encourage us to make use of our dreams. But many people sense that their dreams are important, and aspire to learn about themselves through their dreams.

THE IMPORTANCE
OF DREAMS

Dreams are important because they are real. Dreams are real because they are what we are experiencing at the time. Even when we are dreaming and we realize "this is a dream," that realization is still part of the dream.

Dreams are also important because they give us access to material that is not available to us while we are awake. At night, when our defenses are down, our emotions express themselves freely and in strange configurations. It is the negative emotions such as fear, anger, and hostility that often leave the greatest impression on us when we awaken. One study found that over forty percent of children's dreams dealt with fear and anxiety, and only twenty-two percent dealt with fairy-tale themes (Gereb, Szabo, and Oestreich, 1970). Clearly, the dreamworld is as full of conflict as is daily life, and we should seek ways of resolving these conflicts—both in our waking and our dream lives. However, the dreamworld is also a place where the positive emotions express themselves, and if we can find ways of incorporating this information into our lives, we can use it to achieve an integration of waking and dreaming.

THE SENOI

The Senoi (rhymes with annoy) are a people that live in the Central Malay Peninsula. They consider the dream state real, and they have evolved a set of techniques for working with dreams, which they use with one another every morning.

Although anthropologists had previously studied aspects of Senoi culture, it was the late Kilton Stewart who introduced Senoi dream theory to the outside world in an article published in 1951 (Stewart, 1951). A shortened version of this article was anthologized in *Altered States of Consciousness* (Tart, 1969), and since that time there has been widespread interest in the dream techniques of the Senoi.

Stewart felt that Senoi dream techniques could be beneficial to Western society. Whether or not this is true is an empirical question, of course, but until recently it has been difficult to study the phenomenon because the techniques have been inaccessible and relatively incomplete. We will attempt to remedy that situation by providing a step-by-step sequence of activities that can be used by lay persons and professionals alike.

The Senoi consider the dream state real. Consider for a moment what this means. We think of waking perception as real, so we treat the states of waking perception in certain ways. If we can't resolve an incident in one period of waking perception, we attempt to resolve it another time. We attempt to solve problems while awake, and we carry on social relationships. The Senoi do the same things in their dreams. From early childhood, the Senoi is given techniques to continue and complete dreams, and he uses his dreams not only in his personal development, but as sources of knowledge valuable to him and his fellow Senoi.

This dream-work becomes very important in light of what is known about Senoi society. At the time Kilton Stewart lived among them, there had not been a violent crime reported in Senoi society for two or three hundred years. There was little mental and physical illness among the Senoi, and anxiety among Senoi children largely disappeared by puberty (Stewart, 1951). According to Stewart, the Senoi had the most democratic society ever studied by anthropologists: all decisions were reached by consensus. Because there are other aspects to Senoi culture that could be considered therapeutic, it is not possible to tell whether or not all of the positive aspects of their culture can be attributed to their dream-work, but it seems likely that a daily dream clinic such as the Senoi conduct would have a strong therapeutic effect on a society.

Sundsten reports that although a large percentage of the Senoi are being absorbed into the surrounding Islamic culture, there are still intact tribes in the highlands that carry out dream-work.

SENOI DREAM THEORY

Kilton Stewart summarized Senoi psychology as follows:

> Man creates features or images of the outside world in his own mind as part of the adaptive process. Some of these features are in conflict with him and with each other. Once internalized, these hostile images turn man against himself and against his fellows. In dreams man has the power to see these facets of his psyche, which have been disguised in external forms, associated with his own fearful emotions, and turned against him and the internal images of other people. If the individual does not receive social aid through education and therapy, these hostile images, built up by man's normal

receptiveness to the outside world, get tied together and associated with one another in a way which makes him physically, socially and psychologically abnormal. (Stewart, 1951)

PRINCIPLES OF SENOI DREAM-WORK

The major themes that run through Senoi dream-work are that dreams are real, that dreams should and can be continued and completed, and that completion should result in some knowledge useful to the dreamer and his mates. For example, when a child tells of a falling dream (a common cross-cultural anxiety dream), an adult Temiar tribesman might answer that it was a wonderful dream. If the child says that it did not seem like a wonderful dream at all, the adult suggests again that it was a wonderful dream because it enabled the child to fall "to the source of the power that caused you to fall" (Stewart, 1951). The adult then suggests that the next time such a dream occurs, the child will relax and enjoy himself so that he can learn from the dream. Remarkably, Senoi children learn to do just that.

According to Senoi principles, all dreams of pleasure should be resolved or continued, and the resolution should always yield "something of beauty or use to the group." For example, one should arrive somewhere when he flies, meet the beings there, hear their music, see their designs, and learn their useful knowledge (Stewart, 1951). Frequently, the dreamer learns a song or a poem in the dream that he can share with his friends and family upon awakening.

The Senoi interacts with his mates in and out of the dream state. If a child has a floating, flying, climbing, or traveling dream, he is urged to travel *somewhere* to find things of value to share with his fellows. If he dreams of a fight with a friend, he is urged to apologize to that friend and perhaps present him with a gift. Similarly, group activities are often planned from dream images. If a child dreams of a new hunting device, the adults urge him to try it out, regardless of its practicality. A dream of a new dance will often result in an impromptu tryout of the steps in the morning dream group.

The Senoi have been called technicians of the miraculous. However, the techniques they use are simple enough to be used by any group, family or school. The authors have seen these techniques work in a variety of settings and with age groups ranging from preschoolers to adults.

Techniques for Working
with Dreams[1]

Two prerequisites are important. Much dream-work involves finishing dreams in "the imagination." For this reason, persons who lead dream groups must learn how to guide imagery. Second, participants in dream groups must learn to remember their dreams. Fortunately, neither of these procedures is difficult.

GUIDING IMAGERY

Images are wonderful and mysterious things. Close your eyes and imagine an apple. Can you "see" it? Do you have a small picture of it in front of you that you can see? If so, can you count the blemishes on it? Some

---

[1] Inasmuch as most of this material was originally prepared for use with children's dream groups, most of the examples and references are to children's dreams. The techniques, however, can be used among people of all ages.

people, in other words, can close their eyes and have a vivid image or picture of whatever they want to see. Some people have shifting or partial images, and some do not seem to have this ability at all. Science does not know much about images and how they work, but we know we are capable of creating practically any reality we want by letting our imaginations roam free.

The ability to experience vivid imagery occurs very strongly in children, but it usually wanes as one's age increases. One reason for this decrease in "imagibility" is that it receives very little support and encouragement; another is that imagery is often disapproved outright by adults.

Images are often associated with the creative process. For instance, the chemist Kekulé was working to find the structure of the benzene ring. One night, he had a dream image of a snake eating its own tail. Upon waking, he quickly saw that the structure of the benzene ring indeed resembled a snake eating its own tail. This is one of innumerable examples of collaboration between logical thought and creative imagery.

THE IMAGE STATE

We will refer to that experience in which we close our eyes and sense pictures and sounds as the image state.

When we have an image, we often like to think about it and what it means. To do this we must leave the image state, because thinking involves a different process. So the first task in guiding imagery is to allow the person experiencing imagery to remain in the image state. This is done simply by directing the person's attention to what he is immediately experiencing. The most frequently used question is "What are you seeing now?"

> KAREN: I'm in a tunnel moving along on a . . . it's like . . .
>
> LEADER: Tell us what you're seeing now. Say, "I see . . ."
>
> KAREN: I see . . . oh yeah, I'm on an escalator, moving down past brown walls . . .

Attention is brought back to what the person is seeing and hearing now. Often the images are not *doing* anything.

> KAREN: I'm just seeing blackness.
>
> LEADER: Let yourself feel the blackness. Listen to it.

The second function of the image guide is to help the person move through the image state. This is achieved not by manipulating or controlling the image but, again, by redirecting the person's attention to the immediate experience.

KAREN: I can't see what's in front of me.

LEADER: Feel yourself moving along the escalator, moving slowly forward. Open your imagination just like opening your eyes.

KAREN: I see icicles coming down from the ceiling. It's dark but not scary.

Practice on yourself. Put the book down for a while and close your eyes tightly. Relax them after a few seconds, keeping them closed. What are you seeing now?

REMEMBERING DREAMS

Dream-work is best done in the morning, the earlier the better. We forget dreams the longer we are away from them; then we forget that we forgot them; and then we think we haven't dreamed at all. However, by monitoring brain activity that is known to be associated with dreaming, psychologists have shown us that we all dream every night.

We have found two techniques very helpful in training people to remember their dreams. The first technique is to jot down key dream events on a bedside pad. Persons with a taste for technology can use a cassette tape recorder. With practice, this technique becomes so automatic that the dreamer is sometimes surprised upon awaking to read the content of his nighttime scribbles. An excellent way to facilitate this technique is by self-suggestion. After the person arranges the pad and pencil in a convenient location, he then relaxes, closes his eyes, and makes the following suggestion to himself:

> I will wake up gently and easily after my dreams. I will write the dream quickly, then slip back into sleep. (This is repeated several times.)

The second technique, useful with dreamers of all ages, also makes use of the power of suggestion. Have the children sit in a circle. Sit down with them and begin talking about a dream of your own that you would like to share. Encourage the children to share their dreams. Most children are enthusiastic about this. Be prepared for some far-out stories: because children have not learned to think of one state of consciousness as any more real than another, they sometimes tend to mix incidents from their imagination with incidents from their waking and dream lives.

After a while, say something like this: "We all dream many times a night. Because we want to discuss our dreams more, it would be nice if we began to remember more of them. Several times today you can say to yourself, 'I will remember my dreams when I awaken tomorrow,' and you will be able to remember more of your dreams. Say this several times today, and you will be able to remember your dreams tomorrow."

For the first couple of weeks, the teacher can read the following suggestion exercise, daily if possible. Have the children sit comfortably in a large circle, and read to them:

"Now I want you to feel your pulse and feel how the blood moves through your body. But now I want you to just sit there and feel the pulse of your blood. We can do this by pressing our third and fourth fingers against the sides of our necks and listening (check to see that all of the children have done this)."

Pause (ten seconds)

"Now let's see how our pulse is changed by closing our eyes and lying down and breathing evenly and slowly, evenly and slowly. And now breathe evenly and even more slowly, and be aware of your pulse as it goes slower and slower as you change it by your breathing . . . going slower and slower and slower, in and out, in and out. (Coordinate this breathing sequence, which will be periodically continued for ten seconds each time, with the actual breathing of some child near you.) If you want to, you can become even more aware of your pulse, not in that one place but all over your body, and you can become even more and more and more relaxed and feel your body relaxing and being totally supported by the floor as you breathe in and out, in and out . . . as you listen to my voice and feel your pulse, your blood surging throughout your body, growing even more relaxed as your body relaxes and your pulse relaxes. Relax and breathe deeply and easily, aware of your pulse, your blood moving through your body, aware of my voice, knowing that you don't have to understand what the voice says because you will understand by doing, easily and fully. We dream all the time and always dream every night, and when we do dream as we may be dreaming now, relaxed and attentive, we have only to relax fully in this dreaming and enjoy ourselves fully and see what happens as we are seeing what happens now, relaxed and breathing in and out . . . knowing that we all dream all the time and that it is easy to remember our dreams and that tomorrow morning we will immediately remember what we have dreamed, as much of it as we want to, because all we have to do when we dream is to relax and enjoy ourselves and see what happens, and this is as easy as this is now. All you have to do to remember your dreams is to remind yourself several times during the day that tomorrow morning when you awake you will immediately remember the dreams you have now and that soon when you dream you will remember what is being said to you."

Pause (ten to fifteen seconds)

"Now I am going to count slowly backward from ten

to one, and as I do I want you to leave this state of relaxation, however slowly or quickly you wish, and come back here. Ten, nine, eight, seven, six, five, four, three, two, one, zero—you are fully awake and alert."

CONTINUATION AND COMPLETION OF DREAMS

Just as we should complete unfinished business in our waking lives, we should also attempt to complete situations in our dream lives. We know that leaving matters incomplete can make our waking lives erratic and unsatisfying, and although we cannot directly see the results of unfinished business in our dreams, we can guess that it might have a similar effect. The Senoi believe that unless we complete dreams we cannot become psychologically integrated, and they have thus developed many techniques for the continuation and completion of dreams.

There is, of course, no *right* way to complete a dream. There are only those ways that make us feel good and those that do not. For example, a friend of ours dreamed of seeing a beautiful blue hat on a Buddha. The next night, she tried the Senoi technique of looping (described on p. 79) in order to continue the dream. She dreamed of seeing a large Buddha-like man wailing and crying, and although the content was different from her first dream, she felt that it was a continuation. Our advice is for you to become familiar with the techniques and apply them to your own dream life. Then, as you begin to feel confident enough to work with the dreams of others, center yourself and do what feels right in a given dream situation of your own. Sometimes dreams will be completed in a person's imagination, sometimes in the dream state, other times not at all. One thing is for sure: you won't hurt anyone by the misapplication of these techniques. If you are too far off the mark, the children's interest will simply wane.

On the following pages we discuss several different techniques, arranged in roughly the order in which one might introduce them in a Senoi dream group. We have included examples, taken from actual dream-work sessions, that illustrate points concisely and sometimes dramatically. The reader should rest assured that the authors, and others who do dream-work, make their share of mistakes; we felt, however, that no good purpose would be served by including longer transcripts that showed us bumbling, stumbling, and deftly leading dreamers into cul-de-sacs.

CONTINUATION AND
COMPLETION IN IMAGINATION
WITHOUT A GUIDE

Often, it is best to have a person complete a dream quickly in his own imagination without being guided by the leader. This technique is particularly useful with nonverbal children and with those who do not respond to being guided while in their image state. In the following example, Charles awakened when a dreamworld alligator bit off his toe:

LEADER: Close your eyes and relax, Charlie. *(Pause)* Let yourself get back into the dream. Be right there. *(Pause)* Now go on with the dream from where he bit you. Finish it off. *(Pause; Charles opens his eyes)* Where did you go?

CHARLIE: I got rescued and taken to the hospital. A lady doctor put my toe back on.

LEADER: How do you feel now?

CHARLIE: *(Laughs)* Good.

CONTINUATION AND
COMPLETION THROUGH
GUIDED IMAGERY

In dream-work that involves continuing and completing dreams, this is perhaps the most frequent activity. The goal is that the guide will facilitate the completion of a dream that has been left unfinished. Here are several common incomplete situations, along with suggestions for completing them:

An object is broken—the guide helps the person put it back together.

A person dreams of flying—the guide helps the person to go to the end of the flight, to find out who or what is there, and to bring back something of value to share with the group.

A person dreams of climbing stairs—the guide helps him reach the top.

A dreamer is being attacked—the guide helps him fight the attackers.

A child falls—the guide helps him relax and continue the fall until he falls *somewhere*.

In the following sequence, an elementary teacher guides the imagery of a seven-year-old child named Sybile. The sequence illustrates the points we have been making. Sybile had dreamed repeatedly of playing in a field alone and suddenly seeing an old man observing her. Frightened, she would wake up at this point. Sybile had never done any imagery work before.

TEACHER: Now I want you to relax and close your eyes and see the field that you are playing in, in your dream. Can you do that now? What are you seeing?

SYBILE: I don't see anything. Just a black area with flashes of light coming from the left.

TEACHER: Okay. Now I want you to *pretend* you are seeing that field and pretend you are seeing it now with your eyes closed.

SYBILE: I sort of see it. There is dry grass and a white bare tree with limbs like bones.

TEACHER: How far away from you is the tree?

SYBILE: It's about fifteen or twenty feet in front of me.

TEACHER: And what are you doing? Are you standing up or sitting?

SYBILE: I'm standing looking at the tree.

TEACHER: Okay. Just stand there and look at it and tell me immediately about any changes you notice. *(Pause)* What do you see when you look off to your left?

SYBILE: Just dry grass and sun, and now there are birds moving through the grass.

TEACHER: How far away from you are they?

SYBILE: I don't know. A long way. They're running around in the grass.

TEACHER: Are they aware of you? Can they see you?

SYBILE: I don't know. They are still a long ways away.

TEACHER: Can you see what type of birds they are? What color they are and what shape?

SYBILE: No. They are a long distance away.

TEACHER: Well, one thing we can do with our images is move them in any direction that we want to as fast as we want to, so why don't you move in your images slowly toward the birds until you can see them closer. Go slowly now so you don't frighten them. *(Pause)* Are you doing that?

SYBILE: Yes. I'm getting closer. I can see them now. They are red and brown and seem to be doing some type of dance.

TEACHER: Fine. Why don't you just watch them and see what type of dance they are doing.

SYBILE: There is someone else watching them in the grass. It's the old man. (In this dream imagery, the character we were interested in interacting with appeared spontaneously. One can, of course, have the child *start* the imagery by immediately imagining the person or persons involved in the dream incident in the context of the dream environment.)

TEACHER: How far away from him are you? Can he see you? Is he aware of you?

SYBILE: He can see me and the birds. They have stopped dancing now. (*Long pause where Sybile does not say anything*)

TEACHER: What are you seeing? How do you feel about being with him again?

SYBILE: I feel a little frightened. He is aware of me but he won't look at me. (*Until this point, the teacher has been merely reacting to the sequence of images the child experiences as real, and directing the child's attention toward the images by asking specific orientation questions. At this point, he begins a specific Senoi technique of confronting hostile dream characters, unmasking them, and asking them, "How may I help you?"*)

TEACHER: He can't hurt you. None of these characters can hurt you, so what you can do is go toward him at any rate that is comfortable to you, and force him to look you in the face. Just go toward him slowly; slowly, now, as slow as you want to. And when you get over where you can see him, you can reach up and pull his mask off, and see who it really is. Are you doing that?

SYBILE: I walked toward him and he receded very fast suddenly, and now he is a long way off.

TEACHER: You can move your images as fast as he goes and catch up with him.

SYBILE: I'm up with him again, and he's just sitting there on the ground.

TEACHER: Good. Go over and unmask him now. It looks like he knows he can't get away now.

SYBILE: It's my uncle Max.

TEACHER: Good. Ask him how you can help him. (Pause)

SYBILE: He says I can love him instead of being scared by him when he picks me up and holds me in the air.

PLANNING GROUP ACTIVITIES FROM DREAMS

One of the best ways to get in touch with dreams is to relate dream activities to group activities in the waking state. In the words of Kilton Stewart, if the child dreams "of a new trap, the elders help him to construct it to see if it will work. If he dreams a song or poem, the elders encourage him to express it for criticism and approval" (Stewart, 1951).

These activities can be done individually or in groups. Several examples of each are listed:

GROUP

If a child dreams of a dance or song, he is given the opportunity to lead the group in a performance.

If a child has a dramatic dream, he is encouraged to stage a skit of the dream. He may play the role of participant or director.

If a child dreams a new game, he is urged to play it with the group.

INDIVIDUAL

If a child dreams of a design, he is urged to draw it and then share it with the group.

If a poem is dreamed, it can be set to music to make

a song. If a song is dreamed, it can be played on a classroom instrument.

If an unusual device is dreamed, the child can be encouraged to build it, regardless of its practicality.

If a striking image occurs, it can be the subject of a painting or drawing.

A child can turn almost any dream into a storybook.

CONTINUING DREAMS IN THE DREAM STATE

Senoi children learn at an early age to continue dreams from night to night. Though this skill may seem difficult at first, many young and old dreamers in our culture have been known to learn it very quickly. Two simple techniques have been found useful in helping people return to previous dreams. The first technique involves suggestion, and the second technique, called looping, involves the conscious repetition of certain dream images.

SUGGESTION

The task is to help the individual dreamer make a self-suggestion that the dream will continue. The person should first be helped to relate the dream up to the point at which it stopped. For example, Lucy was on the verge of learning a song from a group of dreamworld bears:

LUCY: . . . and as they were starting to sing, my mother woke me up for school.

LEADER: Okay. You met a group of bears, . . . and they agreed to teach you a song. Then you woke up, right?

LUCY: Yes.

LEADER: Try this tonight just before you go to sleep. Picture the last thing you remember from the dream. What was that?

LUCY: I could see the circle of bears.

LEADER: Good. Picture that and say to yourself, "I will get back into the dream later tonight, and I will learn their song." Say that a few times right now.

Dreamers should be urged to practice the suggestion several times during and after the session, so that even if they forget their nighttime suggestions, there may still be an effect.

As children become familiar with the norms of

dream-work, a subtler type of suggestion begins to work. This type of suggestion could be called "wanting." As children begin to want to continue dreams from night to night, the dreams often begin to occur spontaneously, with no overt suggestion.

LOOPING

Looping is a technique that is done just before sleep. It can be thought of as a form of suggestion, though dream images instead of verbal suggestions are repeated.

This procedure can be continued during the transition from waking to sleeping, slowly looping the last part of a dream sequence in a more and more relaxed manner until one is asleep.

Twelve-year-old Allen had a falling dream that he wished to complete. The leader explains how to do it by looping:

LEADER: Maybe you could tell us what was happening during the last part of the dream?

ALLEN: Mmmmm—I was sort of falling backward through the sky. It happened so fast I'm not sure.

LEADER: Can you remember enough of the feeling to get back into it tonight at bedtime?

ALLEN: I think so.

LEADER: Let's try this. Tonight just before you go to sleep, let yourself get into that feeling, repeating it a few times. Over and over, feel yourself falling. As you repeat it, just relax and go with it wherever it takes you. Okay?

ALLEN: Okay.

LEADER: Let us know what happens.

FALLING DREAMS

Falling dreams are very important to the Senoi. First, they feel that falling dreams are manifestations of anxiety that must be treated, and, second, they believe that falling dreams are a direct route to the source of the spiritual knowledge and power that is available in the world.

The ability to complete a falling dream while asleep takes considerable practice; thus, it is best to begin the completion of falling dreams in the image state, either alone in the dreamer's imagination or with guidance from the leader. The two most effective strategies are *continuing the fall* and *turning falling into flying*.

CONTINUING THE FALL

A falling dream can be completed by assisting the dreamer in continuing the fall that was previously interrupted. The goal is to help the dreamer remain relaxed while falling to the source of the power that is drawing him toward it. When the dreamer completes a fall, he is urged to learn something that is of value to the group.

MIRIAM: . . . I'm falling as if the bed just fell out from under me. Whoosh, and that's all I remember.

LEADER: Falling dreams are really wonderful when we can take some of the scariness out of them. How about leaning back against the cushion to let your body relax. Just get calm, and we'll try to slow down your fall so it won't be scary and you can finish it. Okay. Slip into the feeling of that dream, lying in bed, comfortably asleep. Now feel the bed drop out from under you, and slowly begin to fall. Relax and enjoy the feeling of falling slowly through space. *(Pause)* Fall until you come to the place or thing that's drawing you down, making you fall. *(Pause)* What do you see?

MIRIAM: Blue light.

LEADER: Feel good?

MIRIAM: Mmm-hmmm.

LEADER: See if you can communicate with the light.

MIRIAM: It doesn't say anything.

LEADER: Just feels good.

MIRIAM: Ummm.

LEADER: Good. Let the good feeling of the light flow up through your body, filling you up. *(To group)* Maybe we can all join hands and feel some of that good feeling.

TURNING FALLING
INTO FLYING

As the phrase suggests, this technique attempts to have the dreamer turn a falling dream into a flying adventure. Not only does this take the fear out of the falling experience (usually), but it offers the dreamer an opportunity to fly to some place to learn something of value. Suggestions for turning falling into flying can be made by the dreamer himself during the day or just before sleep, or by the leader during a dream-work session. The following example is a successful attempt to make the transition from falling to flying with a satisfying ending:

TOM: It was like a plane crash.

LEADER: Present tense. (Dreams should be related in the present tense.)

TOM: It feels like a plane crash—like the motors stopped and the plane just dropped straight down.

LEADER: (Gets Tom to relax body) Okay. Relax yourself as you feel that drop. Repeat it a few times, that feeling. *(Pause)* Let yourself fall, and as you do, let the energy from falling turn into flying. Swoop out of the fall into a smooth, soaring flight, like a bird. Are you moving?

TOM: Yes.

LEADER: Through what?

TOM: Space.

LEADER: Move on till you find a place to stop and learn.

TOM: *(Pause)* I can hear the stars singing.

LEADER: Let's hear what it sounds like.

CONTINUITY BETWEEN
DREAMING AND WAKING

Continuity among dreaming, waking, and imagining is a key element in Senoi dream-work, and should be stressed at all times. If a person dreams of slighting another, he goes out of his way to be kind and generous to the slighted person. If a person dreams of injuring anyone he knows, he tells the dream to that person and gives the person a gift such as a drawing, a poem, or a dance. If a person is injured by another during a dream, he tells the person the dream, and the person can then respond with a gift or a kind word.

LUCID DREAMING

A lucid dream is one in which the dreamer knows he is dreaming while he is dreaming. There is an advantage to having this type of awareness, for it facilitates some of the activities described above. For those who like the idea of lucid dreams, and who wish to spend some time cultivating this skill, the description of a technique for lucid dreaming follows.

After one has been aware of and has recorded one's dreams for a week or two, he may begin to notice certain repetitive dream symbols and objects that are very unusual, in the sense that they almost never appear in the dreamer's waking life For example, one child in a preschool where Senoi dream-work was being done would dream repeatedly of the image of a large snake with yellow diamonds on it crawling through a hoop of fire.

After noting and recording these unusual symbols, one then meditates on them repeatedly during the day, bringing the dream image to mind and always noting how unusual it is in the context of waking perception.

In thus associating how unusual such an object is, one is associating a context with the symbol. After one has associated the unusual quality of the symbol with its occurrence for some time, the next time he encounters the symbol in the dream, he has associated the realization "what an unusual symbol this is, how out of my ordinary experience it is" with its occurrence, and then suddenly realizes that the context is not ordinary experience but dreaming. In other words, he realizes that "this is a dream." Once he realizes that the context of the experience is indeed a dream, he immediately has a greater degree of control over what happens in the dream state.

IMAGINING CHARACTERS
FROM DIFFERENT DREAMS
SPEAKING TO EACH OTHER

Sometimes we can combine our dreams and learn

more about them in the process. In the classroom this is
done by having the children relax and imagine they are
sitting quietly, listening to a conversation between characters from two different dreams (or the same dream) and
watching what they do and say and how they interact.
Have the children lie down in comfortable positions, and
then read to them:

"Now I want you to relax and get comfortable as we
have done before, and lay your hands on the ground
beside you. Just begin to relax and let your muscles go
and breathe slowly, in and out and in and out."

Pause

"Breathe slowly now, deeper and deeper, and
become aware of your right hand, supported on the
ground beside you, and all the feelings in that hand that
you can sense. It may feel hot or it may feel cold, but
what is important is that however it feels, you sense as
fully and completely as possible all the feelings in your
right hand, concentrating all your attention now on each
and every feeling that you can sense in the hand."

Pause

"And now become even more aware of your hand
and even more and more relaxed.
And as you relax and let go even more, you may

notice that there are different feelings in different parts of your hand, and all you have to do to become aware of them is to let go and relax even more, now totally concentrating your attention and consciousness on your hand.

Now you are even more relaxed, even deeper and deeper relaxed, and all you have to do is to continue to relax and feel how your right hand feels and how aware of it you are, noticing how easily these feelings come."

Pause

"And now as you become even more aware of your hand, I want you to think of any dream that you have had recently, any dream that you are remembering now or having now, and I want you to remember that dream now, and it is easy to do this and remember that dream, and it may be a dream that you had last night or a dream that you had a long time ago that you have had over and over again, and in this dream that you are remembering and seeing as I am talking, there may be some persons or animals that you would like to see again and watch what they do without them seeing you, and you may not even know who these persons are and you don't even have to know because all you have to do to see them is imagine now that you are hiding in a nice, cozy, comfortable place, the place you most like to be when you hide, and as you lie there feeling your hand, you feel good and secure and cozy because you know that no matter what happens, no one can see you unless you want them to, and you are lying there in this wonderful place where you like to go when you hide."

Pause

"And now as you look up in your images you can see a figure still a long distance away walking toward you, and he is still so far away from you that you cannot yet see who it is as he walks toward you, getting closer and closer and still walking toward where you are lying and hiding, and as he gets closer and closer you can see his face now, the person from your dream now walking toward you, coming closer and closer and finally sitting down a few feet away from you but still unaware that you are there. And as you watch him or her, this person seems to be looking about for someone else, someone he is supposed to meet there and talk with, for although the person cannot see you, you can see him.

And now this person is beginning to rise because you can both see that another dream figure still a long distance away, a very small figure a long distance away, is walking toward both of you, a small tiny figure coming toward you now."

Pause

"And you know as this second person approaches that the person is another character in your dream or another dream, and as you watch this person come nearer and nearer you still cannot see who it is, but you know it is a person from your dream or another dream or any dream you have had or are having now as you watch the person come closer and closer and still closer until both of you can see who it is, and as this person comes closer you can see that it is indeed that person you are dreaming about now getting really near, closer and closer and now sitting down with the other dream character a few feet away from you, and neither of them can see you or are aware of you now as you lie there watching and listening and hearing what they say to each other as they begin to talk, and you lie there and listen."

Pause (one to two minutes)

"And now that you have heard what they said to each other and seen what they did with each other, you can again become aware of your hand there in space as you begin to leave this state of relaxation and come back here.

Now I'm going to count backward slowly from ten to zero, and as I do you will become more and more alert at any rate that is comfortable to you, and when I finish you will be totally alert and awake and able to remember what you have heard and seen, and we will do that now. Ten, nine, eight, seven, six, five, four, three, two, one, zero, totally awake."

If the dreamer has a clear picture of two or more characters with which to interact, there is less need for the lengthy induction presented above. The guide may then simply ask the dreamer to imagine the characters and begin the interchange.

SUMMARY

Senoi dream-work is being used by therapists, teachers, and parents in the Western world to help people integrate their dream lives with their waking lives. We hope that Senoi dream-work will be carried on informally among friends and by teachers and parents.

We probably will never achieve as a society what the Senoi have achieved, but with dream-work techniques perhaps we can help people achieve psychological integration on an individual and a small-group basis. Even if these techniques do not affect our heads at all, at least we will be gathering together to share our very real, and often very beautiful, nighttime creations. Perhaps this in itself is enough.

Hints on Doing Dream-Work

Dream-work has many uses. It can open a fascinating world for educational and family activities, and at the same time help children learn to use one of their major states of consciousness. Dream-work can also be a useful tool in psychological integration. People who work with children's dreams will find their efforts most successful if they remember two important points.

First and foremost, teachers should *avoid interpretation.* Children of all ages (and adults too) love to expand their dreams, act them out, and bring them to completion. Most people, however, become bored when their dreams are interpreted. So, although you may be absolutely sure that Charlie's dreamworld alligator is really his mother, his father, or maybe even you, it is best to leave that kind of speculation to the psychiatrists. There is not much evidence to indicate that interpretation is a useful tool in psychotherapy. We *know* it is a turn-off in the educational process.

Second, teachers should spend considerable time preparing and planning dream sessions. Listen to one teacher describe how she organized dream-work in her classroom:

> First, I found out as much as I could about the Senoi. I read the two Kilton Stewart articles, and shared this information with the class. Then we discussed the Senoi and their way of life. After that I broke the class up into three "tribes" of eight children, then let them begin to share their dreams with one another with almost no help from me. The first sessions were about twenty minutes, and I just floated around from one group to another. I told a few of my dreams to each group. It wasn't until after a couple of weeks that I first *did* anything like a fantasy completion or a group activity.

Although there are many ways to organize dream activities, this teacher found a way that was very successful. For another approach, see Elena Werlin's article, "Movies in the Head" (Werlin, 1971).

6

Imagery

Imagery in Education

Imagery—seeing pictures in the mind—is crucial to education. Imagine trying to read without picturing things; doing a geometry problem without seeing the symbols in your head; or remembering without seeing the important associations. Inasmuch as imagery plays such a large role in education, it is surprising that the typical school curriculum does not contain activities that help students develop this skill. It becomes even more curious when we consider that practically every widely accepted educational goal, from divergent thinking to positive self-image, depends upon imagery.

Imagery can be used to facilitate many types of

learning. For example, one English teacher always heard the cry, "But I don't know what to write about," when she gave creative writing assignments. So she prefaced the next creative writing task with a guided imagery journey. She relaxed the children, then guided them on a mountain hike. Suddenly, they saw a cave leading into the side of the mountain. She left them at the mouth of the cave with instructions to go inside and have an adventure. When they came back, she asked them to write their experiences in two pages. The happy ending to this story is that the only complaints she heard were that two pages were not enough.

Some of the sources in the bibliography at the end of this book contain imagery experiences that may be used for various purposes. Our purpose in the following imagery activities is to build imagery ability and at the same time give students centering experiences that help them feel good.

Finding a Space

This activity will help you and your children find a space all your own to which you can return when you want. Like all imagery experiences, this activity is facilitated by a relaxed body, so if you notice that the children are especially active, you might consider prefacing this with one of the relaxation activities.

INSTRUCTIONS

"Let your body settle down and find a place where it feels comfortable and supported . . . letting all of the tension drain out of your body, letting each breath fill you with peaceful, soothing relaxation."

Pause (ten seconds)

"And now as your body quiets down, let your mind become quiet also. Imagine that your mind is quiet and peaceful, slowing down to a soothing slow pace . . . and as your mind becomes quiet, we will go in our minds to a place where we feel completely safe and secure. This can be a place you already know about, perhaps a room in a house, or it can be a place you build in your mind, but wherever it is, go there now and arrange it just the way you want it to make you feel safe, solid, and secure."

Pause (one to two minutes)

"And now that you have that place, you can go there whenever you want. You can go there to think, to be by yourself even if you're with others, to feel good no matter where you are. Now let's return to the present, knowing that our place will be there when we want it."

Grounding

George Leonard, author of *Education and Ecstasy*, writes of a good example of grounding performed by his eighty-five-pound daughter. After the girl had grounded herself, a weightlifter was unable to lift her. To find out if your children are that good at grounding, try picking one of them up before, during, and after the exercise. You may be surprised. Grounding should be done in a standing position.

INSTRUCTIONS

"Sometimes it feels good to feel yourself connected solidly to the ground, to be part of the earth like a tree.

As you stand here, let your body become comfortable and still, relaxing your shoulders and your legs, moving around a little until you feel a spot that feels good. Close your eyes and feel yourself like a tree growing out of the ground."

Pause (ten seconds)

"Imagine that roots go down deep in the earth below your feet."

Pause (ten seconds)

"Raise your arms and imagine that they are branches and that you are as solidly connected to the earth as a tree."

Pause (ten seconds)

"Feel the energy flow from the tips of your branches down to your roots in the earth."

Pause (ten seconds)

"You can use this feeling of being part of the earth whenever you want to feel solid and connected, whenever you want to feel yourself part of the flow of energy through the earth. Enjoy that feeling for as long as you want now, and then come back to the room at your own speed."

Flower

Everybody loves flowers. But can we feel the beauty of them deep within us?

INSTRUCTIONS

"Close your eyes and tell your muscles to relax. Tell your arms and hands to let go . . . now your legs . . . your chest . . . your face. And as you enjoy the calm feeling of resting in the darkness, imagine a closed flower deep in your mind. And as you imagine this flower, see it slowly begin to open . . . the petals beginning to spread and separate . . . and a beautiful flower opens in your mind. And as your mind becomes filled with the beauty of the flower, you can imagine the rest of the bush: the leaves and branches being your arms, and the roots reaching down through your center into the ground, connecting you solidly with the earth."

Pause (ten seconds)

"And whenever you want to feel good, you can remember the feeling of the flower opening . . . the feeling of the roots connecting you with the ground, helping you feel solid and complete. And now let's return to the present, feeling rested and calm, relaxed and alert."

COMMENTS

Very young children have trouble with this image unless they are familiar with the parts of a flower, such as the petals. One solution to this problem is to combine this imagery experience with a science lesson in which the children learn about parts of flowers.

Light-Centering

Try this activity outdoors in natural light. The standing position is best.

INSTRUCTIONS

"Stand easily, relaxing your body and letting your arms become loose. As your body relaxes, close your eyes and feel the light and warmth of the sun overhead. And now imagine the light coming down into your body through the top of your head."

Pause (five seconds)

"Let it stream down through your head and down your spine."

Pause (five seconds)

"Now let the light shine all the way down your spine."

Pause (five seconds)

"And now feel the light in your center."

Pause (five seconds)

"And now let the light shine out from your center to a few feet in front of you."

Pause (ten seconds)

"And now shine your light until we're all bathed in it."

Pause (thirty seconds)

"And now let's remember this feeling as we return to right now, opening our eyes, and feeling peaceful and calm, rested and alert."

Ripples

This is an imagery experience that takes just a few minutes, but can acquaint you and the children with a feeling of inner stillness to which you can return whenever you want. It can be done sitting or lying down.

INSTRUCTIONS

"We will be taking a journey through inner space, and you can begin by closing your eyes and letting your body relax . . . letting go your toes . . . your feet . . . your legs . . . relaxing your stomach . . . your chest . . . your arms . . . your face . . . your mind . . . and your fingertips. And as you listen to my voice, let it take you deeper and deeper into that feeling of relaxation in which you feel soothed, calm, and peaceful. And as you feel calmer and calmer, imagine that there is a calm, still lake down in the center of your body . . . a peaceful clear lake filled with fresh, still water. And now as you feel still and calm as this lake, drop a pebble into the center of the lake and feel the ripples spreading slowly and smoothly from the center."

Pause (thirty seconds)

"You can return to that feeling of stillness within you whenever you would like to feel still and peaceful. Now let's return our attention to right here, opening our eyes to the light and feeling refreshed and calm."

Imagery Pair

Place the children in groups of two so that they are sitting cross-legged on the ground, facing each other, about four to five feet apart.

INSTRUCTIONS

"This is an activity in which we see our images of others and how these images change.

"Take a few deep breaths and relax. Let your eyes unfocus now, and look at your partner and relax and breathe deeply, in and out and in and out. Now with your eyes still relaxed and gently focused, look at the area between your partner's eyes and see if the two of you can breathe slowly in unison. And now breathe deeply and let your muscles relax with each breath, easily looking and breathing and hearing what is being said, and now just looking for a while."

Pause (one minute)

"And now as you continue to look, you may notice that the edges of your partner's face may begin to alter and move ever so slightly, and that the face may begin to change to other faces you know and have seen or even faces that you have not seen, but all you have to do is relax and continue to breathe deeply and watch the face.

"And these faces may even change into faces of animals, and they may change slowly or quickly, but all you have to do to see them is to continue to sit and relax and watch."

Pause (one minute)

"Now blink your eyes and give your bodies a big stretch."

Synesthesic Imagery

This is a relaxation-imagery activity in which we use our various senses to pick up information we don't normally receive with them. Have the children lie flat on their backs in a relaxed position.

INSTRUCTIONS

"Let's all relax as we have done before, and as you begin to relax, think of all the images of flowers you know if you want to, and all the flowers you have ever seen and smelled and felt, and as you begin to see all these flowers, I want you to relax all your muscles and become comfortable. And now begin that gentle sinking into the floor you are familiar with, totally relaxed and comfortable, and breathing in and out and in and out . . ."

(coordinate this with the breathing rhythm of a child near you).

Pause (fifteen seconds)

"And now become even more relaxed, aware of your entire body, relaxing even more each time your breath goes in and out, relaxing and listening to what I am saying, your entire body listening very closely now and relaxing easily and becoming aware of what the voice is saying as easily as it is to see all the images of flowers you are seeing and all the images of flowers you have ever seen.

"And if you want to now, you can close your eyes on your images, just as we close our eyes while we're awake doing this, and now pretend you are seeing the backs of your eyelids and remember that among all of those flower images that you were seeing there were roses, and there was a rose you can't see now because your eyes are closed, but if you want to you can easily smell it now, very faintly, so why don't you just lie there with your eyes closed and smell that rose, eyes closed and relaxed now, not seeing but merely smelling it as it becomes stronger, smelling this rose.

"And now just lie there for a while, slowly breathing in and out and in and out and smelling this rose."

Pause (fifteen seconds)

"And now your image eyes are still closed, and you are still smelling this faint but definte and stronger smell and hearing this voice and just feeling relaxed and hearing easily what is said to you, just seeing the backs of your eyelids and smelling this rose.

"Now there is something very important for you to hear and know, so you should listen very carefully with your entire body. But all you have to do to do this is to continue to relax with your eyes shut and become more aware of the rose's smell, listening to the voice and relaxing and hearing the voice telling you something very special, for in a while I will tell you to open your image eyes and see this rose you have been smelling and are smelling and have seen but aren't seeing because your image eyes are closed now just as your outside eyes are closed, and when I tell you to open your image eyes, you will be able to see the rose and see the smell of the rose you are now smelling faintly with your eyes closed, emanating from the rose to your body, gently sifting toward you through the air, and when you open your image eyes, you will see the color and texture of the rose and you will see the odor of the rose with your eyes, and I want you to do that NOW.

"See the rose you have been smelling and see the scent you have been smelling. And now see its color and its smell."

Pause

"And now just relax and hold this one rose and its smell in your image eyes, seeing the rose and its smell."

Pause

"Notice that when the voice is not talking, the smell makes a distinct and very soft sound that you can hear, and that part of it comes to your ears just as it comes to your eyes. Now see and hear the smell for a while."

Pause

"Now relax and smell the rose and see its color and texture shine at you and concentrate again on its color, and now if you notice these colors move, you can hear them easily as they do."

Pause

"And now notice the rose's colors moving, and as you listen you can hear the colors moving, and as you see the rose you can feel its smell."

Pause

"You can return to these feelings within you whenever you would like to feel them. And now let's return our attention to right here, feeling calm and alert, opening our eyes NOW."

7

Stretching the Body

Education and the Body

One of the steps in becoming centered is finding ways of dissolving the tension that accumulates in our bodies. If we allow tension to build inside us, we waste energy that we could be using in other ways. Also, if we allow ourselves to develop rigid habits of movement, we decrease our ability to move freely and spontaneously.

Certain types of movements and postures allow us to release tension while moving in ways that dissolve old body habits. Some of these postures come from yoga, some from other sources. These activities are not strenuous, but their value as centering experiences should not be underestimated.

In education, it is important to keep in mind that the students who are solving math problems in their heads are also using the other eighty percent of their beings: their bodies. As we begin to build an education for the whole person, we must pay particular attention to building beneficial styles of movement.

The Stretch

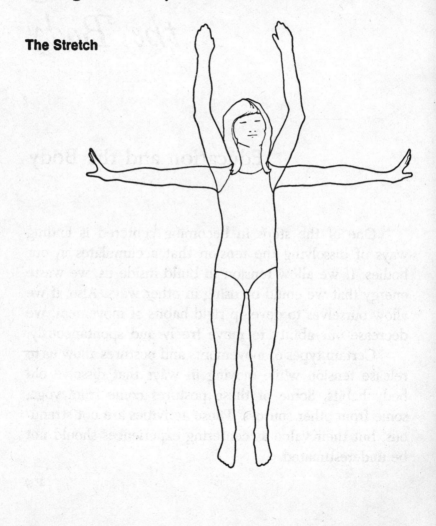

The authors are sometimes challenged on the idea of teaching movement awareness in the classroom, on the ground that physical education already achieves the necessary goals in this area. We reply that movement and body awareness belong in the classroom because students move and use their bodies there. We find that physical education, which has been responsible for developing the body in school, is frequently couched in a competitive context that emphasizes the thrill of victory more than the joy of movement, and its value as a centering experience is thereby decreased.

The Stretch

Doesn't it feel great to stretch? Try this exercise after a period of sedentary activity. Children like it best when it is done to music.

INSTRUCTIONS

"Let's all begin walking slowly around the room, getting the feeling of our bodies in motion. Feel the way we move, the way our feet contact the floor. And as you walk, begin to raise your arms up, stretching as high as you can on each step . . . feeling yourself stretch from your toes to your fingers."

Pause (one minute)

"And now with each slow step, stretch from side to side, bending like a tree in the wind."

Pause (thirty seconds)

"And now bend forward, and walk with your arms hanging loosely, almost to the floor."

Pause (thirty seconds)

"And now take slow, giant steps, stretching your legs."

Pause (thirty seconds)

"And now once more, stretch up to reach the sky."

Pause (ten seconds)

"And now stand still and feel good."

Shaking

This exercise is easy—you just shake. It is particularly enjoyable after a period of inactivity.

Shaking

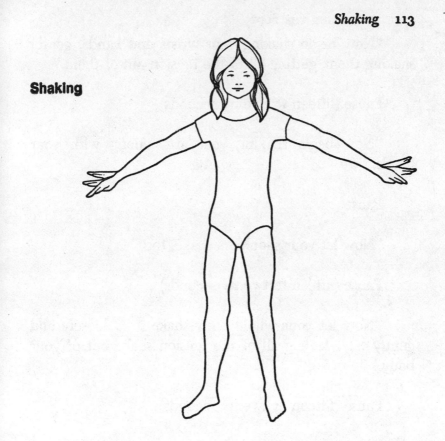

INSTRUCTIONS

"Let's stand loosely and comfortably, moving around until we find a spot that feels good to stand on."

Pause

"Now begin shaking your wrists and hands, gently shaking them, getting all of the tension out of them."

Pause (fifteen to twenty seconds)

"Now begin shaking your arms along with your hands."

Pause

"Now let your shoulders shake, too."

Pause (fifteen to twenty seconds)

"Now let your whole body shake . . . loosely and gently . . . feeling all of the tension shake out of your body."

Pause (fifteen or twenty seconds)

"And now come slowly to a halt . . . take a few deep breaths . . . and center yourself, letting your body become quiet again."

Swinging

This activity stretches the spine gently while giving often-neglected waist muscles a workout.

Swinging

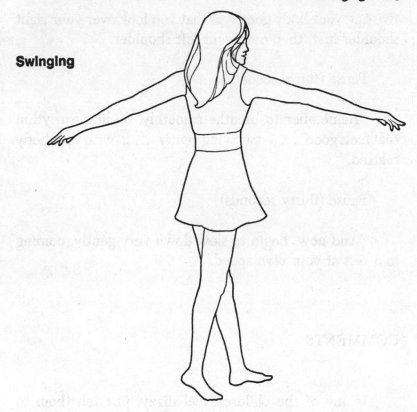

INSTRUCTIONS

"Let's stand straight with our feet about as far apart as our shoulders are wide. Let your arms hang loosely at your sides, and relax your whole body. And as you relax, begin swinging your arms gently from side to side, twisting your body gently so that you look over your right shoulder first, then over your left shoulder."

Pause (thirty seconds)

"Remember to breathe smoothly, finding a rhythm that feels good . . . swinging gently . . . with your body relaxed."

Pause (thirty seconds)

"And now, begin to slow down very gently, coming to a rest at your own speed."

COMMENTS

If any of the children feel dizzy, just tell them to come slowly to a halt and wait until it passes.

The magic words in the following exercises are *smooth*, *gentle*, and *slow*. Sometimes children act silly in these postures, and the silliness comes out in jerky movements. Be patient, but keep reinforcing the performance of smooth, gentle, relaxed movements. Soon, you will see your children lost in the world of their bodies, gently stretching their way to better postures and healthier bodies.

Neck Rotations

Neck Rotations

It is always a good idea to limber up the neck before doing yoga activities. The muscles, nerves, and tendons need warming up before the more strenuous exercises to come. Most people experience some grinding noises in the neck when they first begin to do neck rotations. These noises are normal and will disappear as the neck becomes more flexible. Neck rotations are done in a standing position.

In all of the following postures, avoid strain and competition. If it hurts, stop and do less. And remember, everyone has a different level of flexibility, the only competition is in making ourselves more limber.

INSTRUCTIONS

"Stand comfortably with your body relaxed, and let your arms rise up, outstretched, palms up, straight out from your shoulders. Now lower your head to the right, as if to let your right ear touch your right shoulder."

Pause (five seconds)

"Now let your head drop back as far as it will go, relaxing it and letting your jaw relax."

Pause (five seconds)

"Now lower your head to the left, as if to touch your left ear to your left shoulder."

Pause (five seconds)

"Now let your head drop gently forward, relaxing your neck."

Pause (five seconds)

(Repeat the above directions once or twice.)

"Now roll your head around gently through all the positions, rotating your neck smoothly in a circle."

Pause (fifteen seconds)

"Now go around the opposite way two or three times."

Pause (fifteen seconds)

"Now let your neck come to the center, feeling how it rests gently on the top of your spine, perfectly relaxed and centered. And now stretch from your toes to your fingertips."

Twisting Triangle

Twisting Triangle

INSTRUCTIONS

"Stand up straight, with your body relaxed and comfortable. Raise your arms to shoulder height, your palms facing downward. Breathe in deeply through your nose, and as you exhale, slowly twist your body and bend downward until you grasp your left ankle with your right hand. Exhale all your remaining breath and twist your body further by raising your left arm straight up. Look up at your left hand."

Pause (five seconds)

"Now return slowly to the standing position, breathing deeply as your body comes up."

(Repeat the exercise with the opposite leg. Remind the children to breathe out as they go down and in as they come up.)

Full Bend

INSTRUCTIONS

"Stand straight with your body relaxed. As you breathe in smoothly through your nose, begin raising your

Full Bend

hands high above your head. Stop at the top for a few seconds, then exhale slowly and bend forward with your hands and head until you go down as far as your body wants to go. Stop there for a few seconds, then breathe in and rise back up to a standing position. Remember to keep your legs straight as you go up and down.

(Repeat three or four times.)

The Seated Stretch

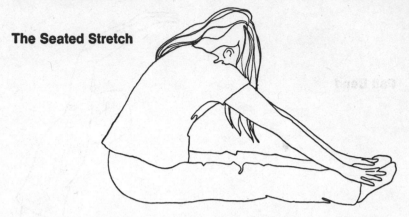

The Seated Stretch

INSTRUCTIONS

"Sit comfortably with both of your legs stretched out in front of you, your arms relaxed at your sides. Breathe in deeply and slowly, raising your arms over your head until your palms come together. Now look up at your hands, and as you begin to breathe out, bend slowly forward from the hips, keeping your legs flat. Stretch your arms out as far as they will go, and as you exhale all your air, reach forward and grasp your ankles or your feet, whichever you can reach. Pull gently, stretching your spine as far as it feels like going. Release your grip and come up slowly, breathing in deeply, bringing your hands back up over your head until the palms touch."

(Repeat two or three times.)

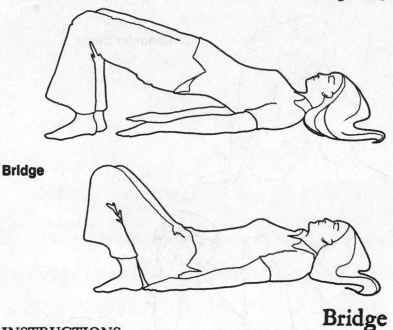

Bridge

Bridge

INSTRUCTIONS

"Lie on your back and relax until you are as flat on the floor as you can be. Draw your knees up until your feet are close to your buttocks. Relax your arms at your sides, palms down on the floor. As you inhale, raise your body gently off the floor by pressing down with your feet. Keep your neck and shoulders relaxed as you arch your back into a bridge. Now exhale and lower yourself to the original position. Relax and let your body sink deeply into the floor."

(Repeat three or four times.)

Shoulder Stand

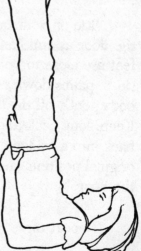

Shoulder Stand

INSTRUCTIONS

"Sit on the floor with your legs drawn up to your chest and your hands on the floor next to your buttocks. Now roll back, bringing your knees over your forehead and sliding your hands under your lower back to support you. Relax in that position, making sure that your back and neck are relaxed. Now begin to raise your legs gently until they are as straight above you as you can get them. Do not strain, but find a position that is straight but not uncomfortable. Relax in this position and breathe deeply, letting all of the unnecessary tension leave your body."

(Have the children hold this position for ten seconds at first, then increase this to one minute.)

"When you're ready to come down, lower your knees slowly to your forehead, then roll your back down to the floor one vertebra at a time, slowly and gently. When you are all the way down to the floor, relax your body completely, feeling yourself totally supported by the floor."

Cobra

Cobra

The Cobra should always be done after the shoulder stand, to stretch the spine in the opposite direction.

INSTRUCTIONS

"Lie on your stomach, stretching your feet out behind you and placing your palms down, next to your armpits. Rest your forehead gently on the floor. Begin to breathe in smoothly, and as you do, begin raising your head, then your neck. As you breathe in more, continue to raise your neck and your spine, without lifting your hips and pelvis, until your chest is off the floor as far as it can go. When you get to the top, relax in that position, then exhale slowly and roll yourself back down until your forehead again touches the floor. Relax your shoulders, your neck, and your back . . . letting yourself sink into the floor."

(Repeat two or three times.)

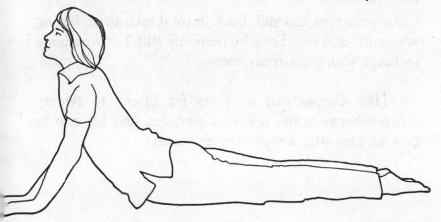

Corpse

The Corpse is used between and after yoga postures.
The alternation between activity and deep relaxation is
important to the success of the exercises we have
described.

INSTRUCTIONS

"Lie on your back on the floor, and let your body
sink down until it is completely supported by the floor.

Corpse

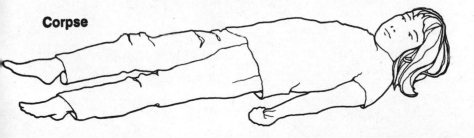

Close your eyes and sink back in total relaxation, letting your mind and your body be perfectly still. Let your body recharge with pure, fresh energy."

(The Corpse can be done for fifteen to twenty seconds between the previous postures, and for one to two minutes after a session of exercises.)

8

Movement and Dance

Movement in Education

Most of the time we walk around in rigid body structures that make us feel tense, and in general we are not aware of the level of tension in our bodies. It is beneficial to get outside those structures so that we can feel our bodies. There are many systems of movement, modern and ancient, that are designed to disrupt our automatic ways of moving so that we can free our bodies of tension. Moshe Feldenkrais, an Israeli teacher of movement, presents a series of exercises in which various muscle structures are moved in the opposite direction from that in which they are normally held. Fingers are bent back from the normal "claw" position, wrists are bent back, the entire body is "opened."

Our need to express ourselves through movement goes far back into man's past. Before there were words there were songs; and before there were songs there was dance, bodies moving together.

Many people all over the world get up every morning and dance with one another in a natural, rhythmic way. In a very fundamental sense, movement is the basis of awareness. Often, what occurs in our consciousness remains obscure and unfelt by us until it reaches our muscle structures. We do not know what is happening in us until our face, body muscles, and breathing muscles arrange themselves into patterns that we recognize as fear, anger, ecstasy, joy, and other feelings. It requires but an infinitesimal amount of time for our muscle structure to rearrange itself in response to an internal state, but we all know it is possible to inhibit our feelings before they become visible to others. We become aware, then, of what is happening in our nervous system when we become aware of such muscle changes. These changes are what most of us can immediately feel.

Sometimes, we become aware of something happening within us but we aren't able to understand what it is. This is a new pattern. But we always act as a whole being even when this wholeness is not perceived and understood, and herein lies the possibility of developing awareness of those parts of the body that we find most difficult to control. In the following section, we present some techniques for doing this.

The Indian yoga systems, developed over thousands of years, are designed to stretch the body in ways that systematically increase flexibility. Less formal types of body movement, such as spontaneous, improvised dance, can be beautiful ways to express feelings.

Movement activities can be done to a background of expressive music. Play an album that conveys the kinds of feelings you would like to help the children get in touch with, or have them bring in some of their favorites. We recommend albums by Santana, Paul Horn, John Fahey, and Ravi Shankar, to name only a few.

In order to avoid stereotypes in the minds of the participants, it is probably best to call these activities something other than "dancing." An alternate term is "movement."

Let us begin with a mandala, or mirror experience.

Mandala[1]

Have the children move into groups of three, facing one another and close enough together so that their hands can touch.

INSTRUCTIONS

"This is a very slow, at first, hand and body game in which one of you begins now to slowly move your arms and hands in whatever slow way you want to, and you can decide now as I'm talking who will begin, and as the leader begins to move, the other two of you will imitate exactly what he or she is doing. Now let's all slowly move our hands and arms and bodies together, feeling everyone moving as you are moving, now beginning to move the entire spine and body . . . swaying together."

(Pause and watch for a while, and then have the children switch leaders and continue until each child has

[1] This movement, along with several others in this section, was developed with help from Kay Ellyard, a California dance therapist. The authors are grateful for her help.

been the leader. When you feel like bringing the movement to a close, have the children switch leaders every three or four seconds until the whole movement dissolves.)

COMMENTS

For longer mandalas, have children focus on different body parts, such as feet or necks. Another possibility is to vary the types of movement the leader performs—strong, weak, fast, slow, shaking, and so forth.

Slow Walking

This activity helps increase awareness of the minute movements of the body. By taking a commonplace activity and slowing it down, we increase our appreciation of the beautiful machine we walk around in every day. Gather the group in a circle.

INSTRUCTIONS

"Our bodies are the most complicated, beautiful, perfect organisms in the world, so let's do something now to make us more aware of how well this organism works. Let's form a line and begin walking in a circle around the room. Just walk as you normally do, paying attention to the movements of your body."

(Go around once or twice.)

"Now slow down your walking so that it takes you two or three minutes to walk around the room. Feel how your feet make contact with the ground, feel the swing of your arms, feel how your joints fit together."

(Go around once.)

"Now move as slowly as your body can. Take a minute or two just to take one step. Feel every muscle your body has to move to take a step."

(Go for three or four minutes, longer if the children are really into it.)

"Now let's stop where we are and center ourselves."

Pause

"Now let's all JUMP FOR JOY."

Revolving from the Center

Gather all the children together in the center of the room.

INSTRUCTIONS

"I'd like you to close your eyes and put your hands at your sides and begin to spin like a slowly spinning top, revolving very slowly with all the other tops all around you and spinning slowly toward the center of the room until you can feel all the other tops spinning slowly and touching you gently, and now spin slowly in and out of the center of the circle, pressing in gently and then being spun out slowly by the other tops."

(Pause one or two minutes while they spin.)

"Now begin to spin and press together harder . . . then gentler again."

Pause

"And now, still spinning slowly and with your eyes closed, bring your hands to the level of your shoulders, and as you revolve, feel the other hands gently touching your hands."

Pause

"And now begin to spin slowly outward, extending your hands slowly as you spin so that you can still feel the other hands as they brush your hands, and now move slowly outward until you have filled the space of the room and your hands are fully extended."

Centering the Body Weight

This movement helps children become more aware of their body weight in relation to gravity. It is done with the children lying on the floor.

INSTRUCTIONS

"Let's close our eyes and feel completely relaxed and feel the earth holding us up, suspending us, for we are completely held and supported by the earth. Feel yourself giving over to this feeling of being held by the earth, relaxing and feeling your body resting heavily on the earth, firmly supported and even more relaxed."

Pause

"And now feel even more relaxed, and if you want you can feel or see your bones supporting you as you lie firmly supported by the earth. Feel the bones inside your body, supporting you as you are supported by the earth, these bones that support you as you move around."

Pause

"Feel your foot bones move slowly around, and now feel each of the little bones in each of your toes beginning to wiggle slowly. You are still relaxed now, feeling all the tiny bones in your foot and feeling all of your big heavy bones resting on the floor supporting you as you feel even more relaxed and comfortable, and now thinking of all the bones in each of your toes, and how they are connected to your feet, and feeling the heel bones resting on the floor, and letting yourself be completely relaxed.

Now go up into your ankles and legs and imagine the insides of your calves. Feel your calf muscles under your shinbones, and imagine you can see how your knees are made, all relaxed now with the earth supporting you."

Pause

"And now feel and see your big thighbone as it fits into your hip socket . . . and imagine your pelvis like a bowl. And now slip your hands along the floor and touch the shape of your hipbones and pelvic bones . . . feeling how comfortable it is to be completely supported by the earth."

Pause

"And now imagine the little tail at the beginning of your spine . . . all the little bones . . . and move up along your spine, vertebra by vertebra, until you feel the beginnings of your ribs. And now feel how your whole skeleton and body is being supported by the earth."

Pause

"Feel now the interaction of your back and the earth as you breathe, and become more aware of the way your body changes as you breathe. And now feel the weight of your shoulder blades on the earth, and imagine your collarbones, seeing if they are completely relaxed."

Pause

"Moving out into your arms now, feel the way your arm bones fit into the shoulder sockets and feel that joint being completely relaxed now that the earth is supporting you."

Pause

"And now imagine your elbow joint bent a little, and relaxed. Feel how your arm moves into a wrist and spreads out suddenly to become a hand. And now see and feel all of the tiny bones of your hand slowly beginning to move, the fingers wiggling, and feel them completely supported by the earth."

Pause

"Feeling all of your body relaxed and rested, let yourself come back to the present, gradually becoming more and more alert, letting the feeling of rested alertness come into your body. When you are ready, sit up, feeling relaxed and calm."

Palm Tree Sway

This is a series of movements in which we can become more aware of our body weight. Form a large circle, leaving enough room between children so that their hands may be extended without touching.

INSTRUCTIONS

"Let's plant our feet into the earth slightly apart and feel like we have roots there, feeling like a palm tree in the desert with a little wind slowly moving our heads and leaving our bodies straight."

Pause

"And now sway all of your upper body from your waist, moving your arms and head and chest, twisting your body above the waist."

Pause

"And now sway yourself from your pelvis, knees straight . . . and now sway yourself from your knees . . . and now from your ankles. Feel the center of movement move from your feet up through your ankles into your knees . . . then into your hips . . . then into your waist. Feel the movement center up and down your body."

Pause

"And now sit slowly on the floor cross-legged and sway back and forth, feeling your hipbones firm and hard underneath, keeping your head and neck loose, tipping forward and backward from your feet to your hipbones."

Pause

"Now rock on your back, holding your knees loosely, rocking from side to side."

Pause

"And now sit up until you are sitting again on your hipbones, cross-legged, swaying in small circles at first, then making them bigger and bigger . . . then smaller and smaller, until you are making just the tiniest of circles."

Pause

"And now let yourself come to rest, completely still and centered, feeling peaceful and attentive."

9

Storytelling

Although stories are commonly read to young children, in school and at home, the following stories can enrich the lives of people of all ages. This is because the stories speak to every person in a different way. For some, these stories may simply be enjoyable; for others, they may communicate a meaning that transcends entertainment. The Sufis, an ancient organization dedicated to psychological and spiritual development, have used stories like these for centuries as exercises in self-awareness.

These are stories for the whole person, for the listener is most rewarded when he gives himself up wholly to the story, to be carried along by the richness of the imagery. When the storyteller is as lost in the story as the listener, there is magic in the air.

Storytelling is nearly a lost art, replaced by flashier

but often less fulfilling media such as television. It is our hope that stories such as these will reacquaint children and adults alike to the joys of good stories well told.*

The Magic Horse

Once upon a time—not so very long ago—there was a realm in which the people were exceedingly prosperous. All kinds of discoveries had been made by them, in the growing of plants, in harvesting and preserving fruits, and in making objects for sale to other countries: and in many other practical arts.

Their ruler was unusually enlightened, and he encouraged new discoveries and activities, because he knew of their advantages for his people.

He had a son named Hoshyar, who was expert in using strange contrivances, and another—called Tambal —a dreamer, who seemed interested only in things which were of little value in the eyes of the citizens.

From time to time the king, who was named King Mumkin, circulated announcements to this effect:

* Permission to reprint "The Magic Horse," "The Tale of the Sands," and "The Man, the Snake, and the Stone," from Idries Shah's *Caravan of Dreams* (London: Octagon Press) is granted by the publisher. © Idries Shah.

Let all those who have notable devices and useful artifacts present them to the palace for examination, so that they may be appropriately rewarded.

Now there were two men of that country—an ironsmith and a woodworker—who were great rivals in most things, and each delighted in making strange contraptions. When they heard this announcement one day, they agreed to compete for an award, so that their relative merits could be decided once and for all, by their sovereign, and publicly recognized.

Accordingly, the smith worked day and night on a mighty engine, employing a multitude of talented specialists, and surrounding his workshop with high walls so that his devices and methods should not become known.

At the same time the woodworker took his simple tools and went into a forest where, after long and solitary reflection, he prepared his own masterpiece.

News of the rivalry spread, and people thought that the smith must easily win, for his cunning works had been seen before, and while the woodworker's products were generally admired, they were only of occasional and undramatic use.

When both were ready, the king received them in open court.

The smith produced an immense metallic fish which could, he said, swim in and under the water. It could carry large quantities of freight over the land. It could burrow into the earth; and it could even fly slowly through the air. At first the court found it hard to believe that there could be such a wonder made by man: but when the smith and his assistants demonstrated it, the king was overjoyed and declared the smith among the most honoured in the land, with a special rank and the title of "Benefactor of the Community."

Prince Hoshyar was placed in charge of the making of the wondrous fishes, and the services of this new device became available to all mankind.

Everyone blessed the smith and Hoshyar, as well as the benign and sagacious monarch whom they loved so much.

In the excitement, the self-effacing carpenter had been all but forgotten. Then, one day, someone said: "But what about the contest? Where is the entry of the woodworker? We all know him to be an ingenious man. Perhaps he has produced something useful."

"How could anything possibly be as useful as the Wondrous Fishes?" asked Hoshyar. And many of the courtiers and the people agreed with him.

But one day the king was bored. He had become accustomed to the novelty of the fishes and the reports of the wonders which they so regularly performed. He said: "Call the woodcarver, for I would now like to see what he has made."

The simple woodcarver came into the throne-room, carrying a parcel, wrapped in coarse cloth. As the whole court craned forward to see what he had, he took off the covering to reveal—a wooden horse. It was well enough carved, and it had some intricate patterning chiseled into it, as well as being decorated with coloured paints but it was only . . . "A mere plaything!" snapped the king.

"But, Father," said Prince Tambal, "let us ask the man what it is for."

"Very well," said the king, "what is it for?"

"Your majesty," stammered the woodcarver, "it is a magic horse. It does not look impressive, but it has, as it were, its own inner senses. Unlike the fish, which has to be directed, this horse can interpret the desires of the rider, and carry him wherever he needs to go."

"Such a stupidity is fit only for Tambal," murmured the chief minister at the king's elbow. "It cannot have any real advantage when measured against the wondrous fish."

The woodcarver was preparing sadly to depart when Tambal said: "Father, let me have the wooden horse."

"All right," said the king, "give it to him. Take the woodcarver away and tie him on a tree somewhere, so that he will realize that our time is valuable. Let him contemplate the prosperity which the wondrous fish has brought us, and perhaps after some time we shall let him go free, to practice whatever he may have learned of real industriousness, through true reflection."

The woodcarver was taken away, and Prince Tambal left the court carrying the magic horse.

Tambal took the horse to his quarters, where he discovered that it had several knobs, cunningly concealed in the carved designs. When these were turned in a certain manner, the horse—together with anyone mounted on it—rose into the air and sped to whatever place was in the mind of the person who moved the knobs.

In this way, day after day, Tambal flew to places which he had never visited before. By this process he came to know a great many things. He took the horse everywhere with him.

One day he met Hoshyar, who said to him: "Carrying a wooden horse is a fit occupation for such as you. As for me, I am working for the good of all, towards my heart's desire!"

Tambal thought: "I wish I knew what was the good of all. And I wish I could know what my heart's desire is."

When he was next in his room, he sat upon the horse and thought: "I would like to find my heart's desire." At the same time he moved some of the knobs on the horse's neck.

Swifter than light the horse rose into the air and carried the prince a thousand days' ordinary journey away, to a far kingdom, ruled by a magician-king.

The king, whose name was Kahana, had a beautiful daughter called Precious Pearl, Durri-Karima. In order to protect her, he had imprisoned her in a circling palace, which wheeled in the sky, higher than any mortal could reach. As he was approaching the magic land, Tambal saw the glittering palace in the heavens, and alighted there.

The princess and the young horseman met and fell in love.

"My father will never allow us to marry," she said; "for he has ordained that I become the wife of the son of another magician-king who lives across the cold desert to the east of our homeland. He has vowed that when I am old enough I shall cement the unity of the two kingdoms by this marriage. His will has never been successfully opposed."

"I will go and try to reason with him," answered Tambal, as he mounted the magic horse again.

But when he descended into the magic land there were so many new and exciting things to see that he did not hurry to the palace. When at length he approached it, the drum at the gate, indicating the absence of the king, was already beating.

"He has gone to visit his daughter in the Whirling Palace," said a passer-by when Tambal asked him when the king might be back; "and he usually spends several hours at a time with her."

Tambal went to a quiet place where he willed the horse to carry him to the king's own apartment. "I will approach him at his own home," he thought to himself, "for if I go to the Whirling Palace without his permission he may be angry."

He hid behind some curtains in the palace when he got there, and lay down to sleep.

Meanwhile, unable to keep her secret, the Princess Precious Pearl had confessed to her father that she had been visited by a man on a flying horse, and that he wanted to marry her. Kahana was furious.

He placed sentries around the Whirling Palace, and returned to his own apartment to think things over. As soon as he entered his bedchamber, one of the tongueless magic servants guarding it pointed to the wooden horse lying in a corner. "Aha!" exclaimed the magician-king. "Now I have him. Let us look at this horse and see what manner of thing it may be."

As he and his servants were examining the horse, the prince managed to slip away and conceal himself in another part of the palace.

After twisting the knobs, tapping the horse, and generally trying to understand how it worked, the king was baffled. "Take that thing away. It has no virtue now, even if it ever had any," he said. "It is just a trifle, fit for children."

The horse was put into a store-cupboard.

Now King Kahana thought that he should make arrangements for his daughter's wedding without delay, in case the fugitive might have other powers or devices with which to try to win her. So he called her to his own palace and sent a message to the other magician-king, asking that the prince who was to marry her be sent to claim his bride.

Meanwhile Prince Tambal, escaping from the palace by night when some guards were asleep, decided that he must try to return to his own country. His quest for his heart's desire now seemed almost hopeless. "If it takes me the rest of my life," he said to himself, "I shall come back here, bringing troops to take this kingdom by force. I can only do that by convincing my father that I must have his help to attain my heart's desire."

So saying, he set off. Never was a man worse equipped for such a journey. An alien, traveling on foot, without any kind of provisions, facing pitiless heat and freezing nights interspersed with sandstorms, he soon became hopelessly lost in the desert.

Now in his delirium, Tambal started to blame himself, his father, the magician-king, the woodcarver, even the princess and the magic horse itself. Sometimes he thought he saw water ahead of him, sometimes fair cities, sometimes he felt elated, sometimes incomparably sad. Sometimes he even thought that he had companions in his difficulties, but when he shook himself he saw that he was quite alone.

He seemed to have been traveling for an eternity. Suddenly, when he had given up and started again several times, he saw something directly in front of him. It looked like a mirage: a garden, full of delicious fruits, sparkling and almost, as it were, beckoning him towards them.

Tambal did not at first take much notice of this, but soon as he walked, he saw that he was indeed passing through such a garden. He gathered some of the fruits and tasted them cautiously. They were delicious. They took away his fear as well as his hunger and thirst. When he was full, he lay down in the shade of a huge and welcoming tree and fell asleep.

When he woke up he felt well enough, but something seemed to be wrong. Running to a nearby pool, he looked at his reflection in the water. Staring up at him was a horrible apparition. It had a long beard, curved horns, ears a foot long. He looked down at his hands. They were covered with fur.

Was it a nightmare? He tried to wake himself, but all the pinching and pummelling had no effect. Now, almost bereft of his senses, beside himself with fear and horror, thrown into transports of screaming, racked with sobs, he threw himself on the ground. "Whether I live or die," he thought, "these accursed fruits have finally ruined me. Even with the greatest army of all time, conquest will not help me. Nobody would marry me now, much less the Princess Precious Pearl. And I cannot imagine the beast who would not be terrified at the sight of me—let alone my heart's desire!" And he lost consciousness.

When he woke again, it was dark and a light was approaching through the groves of silent trees. Fear and hope struggled in him. As it came closer he saw that the light was from a lamp enclosed in a brilliant starlike shape, and it was carried by a bearded man, who walked in the pool of brightness which it cast around.

The man saw him. "My son," he said, "you have been affected by the influences of this place. If I had not come past, you would have remained just another beast of this enchanted grove, for there are many more like you. But I can help you."

Tambal wondered whether this man was a fiend in disguise, perhaps the very owner of the evil trees. But, as his sense came back he realized that he had nothing to lose.

"Help me, father," he said to the sage.

"If you really want your heart's desire," said the other man, "you have only to fix this desire firmly in your mind, not thinking of the fruit. You then have to take up some of the dried fruits, not the fresh, delicious ones, lying at the foot of all these trees, and eat them. Then follow your destiny."

So saying, he walked away.

While the sage's light disappeared into the darkness, Tambal saw that the moon was rising, and in its rays he could see that there were indeed piles of dried fruits under every tree.

He gathered some and ate them as quickly as he could.

Slowly, as he watched, the fur disappeared from his hands and arms. The horns first shrank, then vanished. The beard fell away. He was himself again. By now it was first light, and in the dawn he heard the tinkling of camel bells. A procession was coming through the enchanted forest.

It was undoubtedly the cavalcade of some important

personage, on a long journey. As Tambal stood there, two outriders detached themselves from the glittering escort and galloped up to him.

"In the name of the prince, our lord, we demand some of your fruit. His celestial Highness is thirsty and has indicated a desire for some of these strange apricots," said an officer.

Still Tambal did not move, such was his numbed condition after his recent experiences. Now the prince himself came down from his palanquin and said:

"I am Jadugarzada, son of the magician-king of the East. Here is a bag of gold, oaf. I am having some of your fruit, because I am desirous of it. I am in a hurry, hastening to claim my bride, Princess Precious Pearl, daughter of Kahana, magician-king of the West."

At these words Tambal's heart turned over. But, realizing that this must be his destiny which the sage had told him to follow, he offered the prince as much of the fruit as he could eat.

When he had eaten, the prince began to fall asleep. As he did so, horns, fur, and huge ears started to grow out of him. The soldiers shook him, and the prince began to behave in a strange way. He claimed that he was normal, and that they were deformed.

The counselors who accompanied the party restrained the prince and held a hurried debate. Tambal claimed that all would have been well if the prince had not fallen asleep. Eventually it was decided to put Tambal in the palanquin to play the part of the prince.

The horned Jadugarzada was tied to a horse with a veil thrown over his face, disguised as a serving-woman.

"He may recover his wits eventually," said the counselors, "and in any case he is still our prince. Tambal shall marry the girl. Then, as soon as possible, we shall carry them all back to our own country for our king to unravel the problem."

Tambal, biding his time and following his destiny, agreed to his own part in the masquerade.

When the party arrived at the capital of the West, the king himself came out to meet them. Tambal was taken to the princess as her bridegroom, and she was so astonished that she nearly fainted. But Tambal managed to whisper to her rapidly what had happened, and they were duly married, amid great jubilations.

In the meantime the horned prince had half recovered his wits, but not his human form, and his escort still kept him under cover. As soon as the feasting was over, the chief of the horned prince's party (who had been keeping Tambal and the princess under a very close watch) presented himself to the court. He said: "O just and glorious monarch, fountain of wisdom; the time has now come, according to the pronouncements of our astrologers and soothsayers, to conduct the bridal pair back to our own land, so that they may be established in their new home under the most felicitous circumstances and influences."

The princess turned to Tambal in alarm, for she knew that Jadugarzada would claim her as soon as they

were on the open road—and make an end of Tambal in
the bargain.

Tambal whispered to her, "Fear nothing. We must
act as best we can, following our destiny. Agree to go,
making only the condition that you will not travel
without the wooden horse."

At first the magician-king was annoyed at this foible
of his daughter's. He realized that she wanted the horse
because it was connected with her first suitor. But the
chief minister of the horned prince said: "Majesty, I
cannot see that this is anything worse than a whim for a
toy, such as any young girl might have. I hope that you
will allow her to have her plaything, so that we may make
haste homeward."

So the magician-king agreed, and soon the cavalcade
was resplendently on its way. After the king's escort had
withdrawn, and before the time of the first night-halt, the
hideous Jadugarzada threw off his veil and cried out to
Tambal:

"Miserable author of my misfortunes! I now intend
to bind you hand and foot, to take you captive back to my
own land. If, when we arrive there, you do not tell me
how to remove this enchantment, I will have you flayed
alive, inch by inch. Now, give me the Princess Precious
Pearl."

Tambal ran to the princess and, in front of the
astonished party, rose into the sky on the wooden horse
with Precious Pearl mounted behind him.

Within a matter of minutes the couple alighted at

the palace of King Mumkin. They related everything that had happened to them, and the king was almost overcome with delight at their safe return. He at once gave orders for the hapless woodcarver to be released, recompensed, and applauded by the entire populace.

When the king was gathered to his fathers, Princess Precious Pearl and Prince Tambal succeeded him. Prince Hoshyar was quite pleased, too, because he was still entranced by the wondrous fish.

"I am glad for your own sakes, if you are happy," he used to say to them, "but, for my own part, nothing is more rewarding than concerning myself with the wondrous fish."

And this history is the origin of a strange saying current among the people of that land, yet whose beginnings have now been forgotten. The saying is: "Those who want fish can achieve much through fish, and those who do not know their heart's desire may first have to hear the story of the wooden horse."

The Tale of the Sands

A bubbling stream reached a desert, and found that it could not cross it. The water was disappearing into the fine sand, faster and faster. The Stream said aloud, "I want to cross this desert, but I can see no way."

The voice of the Desert answered, in the hidden tongue of nature, saying, "The Wind crosses the desert, and so can you."

"But, whenever I try, I am absorbed into the sand; and even if I dash myself at the desert, I can only go a little distance."

The voice of the Desert said, "The Wind does not dash itself against the desert sand."

"But the Wind can fly, and I cannot."

"You are thinking in the wrong way; trying to fly by yourself is absurd. Allow the Wind to carry you over the sand."

"But how can that happen?"

"Allow yourself to be absorbed in the Wind."

The Stream protested that it did not want to lose its individuality in that way. If it did, it might not exist again.

Said the Voice, when the Wind absorbed moisture, it carried it over the desert, and then let it fall again like rain. The rain again became a river.

But how, asked the Stream, could it know that this was true?

"It is so, and you must believe it, or you will simply be sucked down by the sands to form, after several million years, a quagmire."

"But if that is so, will I be the same river that I am today?"

"You cannot in any case remain the same stream that you are today. The choice is not open to you; it only seems to be open. The Wind will carry your essence, the finer part of you. When you become a river again at the mountains beyond the sands, men may call you by a different name; but you yourself, essentially, will know that you are the same. Today you call yourself such and such a river only because you do not know which part of it is even now your essence."

So the Stream crossed the desert by raising itself into the arms of the welcoming Wind, which gathered it slowly and carefully upward, and then let it down with gentle firmness, atop the mountains of a far-off land. "Now," said the Stream, "I have learned my true identity."

But it had a question, which it bubbled up as it sped along: "Why could I not reason this out on my own; why did the Sands have to tell me? What would have happened if I had not listened to the Sands?"

Suddenly a small voice spoke to the Stream. It came from a grain of sand. "Only the Sands know, for they have seen it happen; moreover, they extend from the river to the mountain. They form the link, and they have their function to perform, as has everything. The way in which the stream of life is to carry itself on its journey is written in the Sands."

The Man, the Snake,
and the Stone

One day a man who had not a care in the world was walking along a road. An unusual object to one side of him caught his eye. "I must find out what this is," he said to himself.

As he came up to it, he saw that it was a large, very flat stone.

"I must find out what is underneath this," he told himself. And he lifted the stone.

No sooner had he done so than he heard a loud, hissing sound, and a huge snake came gliding out from a hole under the stone. The man dropped the stone in alarm. The snake wound itself into a coil, and said to him:

"Now I am going to kill you, for I am a venomous snake."

"But I have released you," said the man. "How can you repay good with evil? Such an action would not accord with reasonable behaviour."

"In the first place," said the snake, "you lifted the

stone from curiosity and in ignorance of the possible consequences. How can this now suddenly become 'I have released you'?"

"We must always try to return to reasonable behaviour, when we stop to think," murmured the man.

"Return to it when you think invoking it might suit your interests," said the snake.

"Yes," said the man, "I was a fool to expect reasonable behaviour from a snake."

"From a snake, expect snake-behaviour," said the snake. "To a snake, snake-behaviour is what can be regarded as reasonable."

"Now I am going to kill you," it continued.

"Please do not kill me," said the man, "give me another chance. You have taught me about curiosity, reasonable behaviour, and snake-behaviour. Now you would kill me before I can put this knowledge into action."

"Very well," said the snake, "I shall give you another chance. I shall come along with you on your journey. We will ask the next creature whom we meet, who shall be neither a man nor a snake, to adjudicate between us."

The man agreed, and they started on their way.

Before long they came to a flock of sheep in a field. The snake stopped, and the man cried to the sheep:

"Sheep, sheep, please save me! This snake intends to kill me. If you tell him not to do so he will spare me. Give a verdict in my favour, for I am a man, the friend of sheep."

One of the sheep answered:

"We have been put out into this field after serving a man for many years. We have given him wool year after year, and now that we are old, tomorrow he will kill us for mutton. That is the measure of the generosity of men. Snake, kill that man!"

The snake reared up and his green eyes glittered as he said to the man: "This is how your friends see you. I shudder to think what your enemies are like!"

"Give me one more chance," cried the man in desperation. "Please let us find someone else to give an opinion, so that my life may be spared."

"I do not want to be as unreasonable as you think I am," said the snake, "and I will therefore continue in accordance with your pattern, and not with mine. Let us ask the next individual whom we may meet—being neither man nor a snake—what your fate is to be."

The man thanked the snake, and they continued on their journey.

Presently they came upon a lone horse, standing hobbled in a field. The snake addressed him:

"Horse, horse, why are you hobbled like that?"

The horse said:

"For many years I served a man. He gave me food, for which I had not asked, and he taught me to serve him. He said that this was in exchange for the food and stable. Now that I am too infirm to work, he has decided to sell me soon for horse-meat. I am hobbled because the man thinks that if I roam over this field I will eat too much of his grass."

"Do not make this horse my judge, for God's sake!" exclaimed the man.

"According to our compact," said the snake inexorably, "this man and I have agreed to have our case judged by you."

He outlined the matter, and the horse said:

"Snake, it is beyond my capabilities and not in my nature to kill a man. But I feel that you, as a snake, have no alternative but to do so if a man is in your power."

"If you will give me just one more chance," begged the man, "I am sure that something will come to my aid. I have been unlucky on this journey so far, and have only come across creatures who have a grudge. Let us therefore choose some animal which has no such knowledge and hence no generalized animosity toward my kind."

"People do not know snakes," said the snake, "and yet they seem to have a generalized animosity toward them. But I am willing to give you just one more chance."

They continued their journey.

Soon they saw a fox, lying asleep under a bush beside the road. The man woke the fox gently, and said:

"Fear nothing, brother fox. My case is such-and-such, and my future depends upon your decision. The snake will give me no further chance, so only your generosity or altruism can help me."

The fox thought for a moment, and then he said:

"I am not sure that only generosity or altruism can operate here. But I will engage myself in this matter. In order to come to a decision I must rely upon something more than hearsay. We must demonstrate as well. Come, let us return to the beginning of your journey, and examine the facts on the spot."

They returned to where the first encounter had taken place.

"Now we will reconstruct the situation," said the fox; "snake, be so good as to take your place once more, in your hole under that flat stone."

The man lifted the stone, and the snake coiled itself up in the hollow beneath it. The man let the stone fall.

The snake was now trapped again, and the fox, turning to the man, said: "We have returned to the beginning. The snake cannot get out unless you release him. He leaves our story at this point."

"Thank you, thank you," said the man, his eyes full of tears.

"Thanks are not enough, brother," said the fox. "In addition to generosity and altruism there is the matter of my payment."

"How can you enforce payment?" asked the man.

"Anyone who can solve the problem which I have just concluded," said the fox, "is well able to take care of such a detail as that. I again invite you to recompense me, from fear if not from any sense of justice. Shall we call it, in your words, being 'reasonable'?"

The man said:

"Very well, come to my house and I will give you a chicken."

They went to the man's house. The man went into his chicken-coop, and came back in a moment with a bulging sack. The fox seized it and was about to open it when the man said:

"Friend fox, do not open the sack here. I have human neighbours and they should not know that I am co-operating with a fox. They might kill you, as well as censuring me."

"That is a reasonable thought," said the fox. "What do you suggest I do?"

"Do you see that clump of trees yonder?" said the man, pointing.

"Yes," said the fox.

"You run with the sack into that cover, and you will be able to enjoy your meal unmolested."

The fox ran off.

As soon as he reached the trees a party of hunters, whom the man knew would be there, caught him. He leaves our story here.

And the man? His future is yet to come.

References

LINDEN, WILLIAM. The relation between the practicing of meditation by schoolchildren and their levels of field dependence-independence, test anxiety and reading achievement. *Dissertation Abstracts International*, 1972 (Oct.) Vol. 33 (4-B) 1798.

STEWART, KILTON. Dream theory in Malaya. *Complex*, 1951, 6, 21–34.

TART, CHARLES. *Altered States of Consciousness*. New York: Wiley, 1969.

WERLIN, ELENA. Movies in the head. *K-Eight*, Nov.-Dec., 1971, 36–52.

Questions from Teachers and Parents

Using *The Centering Book*

1. *What is centering all about, and how can it help me work with children?*

Schools are changing rapidly. They were once concerned only with intellectual development, but now most schools recognize that social and emotional processes are crucial to children's development. Centering helps children form a union of their intellectual, social, emotional, and spiritual potentials, so that they can be more responsive to their environment.

The last decade has seen an increase in the practice of meditation, yoga, psychosynthesis, Gestalt therapy, and other growth techniques. The goal of these techniques is to help us integrate our mind and body so that we can maintain our psychological center of gravity. We believe it is time to bring centering techniques into wide use in our schools and homes. It is our hope that these techniques will help children form a more perfect union of their powers while helping to prevent the disintegration of this union with which we are all born.

2. *What age groups can use centering activities?*

These activities can be used by all age groups from preschool to high school. (The authors have also used the activities with teachers and parents.) Some of the activities must be adapted slightly to meet the needs of different groups, but the teacher will find these adaptations easy to make.

3. *Is there a special order in which these activities should be done?*

The order in which the activities appear in this book is a good order, but your own order would be just as good. However, it would be helpful for you to read the whole book before you begin using the activities.

4. *How can I organize the activities?*

One method that teachers have used is to set aside fifteen or twenty minutes each day for them. Of course, some teachers intersperse their whole day with activities like these, but a good way to start would be to take a few minutes each day at a time when you sense that the energy of the children is low or undirected.

5. *Should I participate in the activities along with the children?*

By all means. It is essential that you do. You can lead the activities, or you can have one of the children lead, but you should always participate along with the students.

6. *What should I do if the children act silly when I'm trying to get these activities going?*

First, love yourself for feeling up tight, because being up tight is part of life. Then center yourself and say something like this: "I feel up tight when you kids act silly when I'm trying to be serious." Or you might say, "It feels silly doing this, doesn't it?" Or you might just center yourself and try to start the activity again.

When these activities are introduced, there is usually some initial silliness. Then the techniques begin to create their own discipline, and the teacher doesn't have to worry about it anymore. A study (Linden, 1973) was done in which meditation was taught to children in a New York public school. The population of the school was half black and half Puerto Rican, and constituted a very aggressive environment. Even in this school, the techniques were successful. Once some initial silliness subsided, the children responded very well.

7. *What should I call these activities?*

Ask the children to pick a name. They tend to come up with names such as "quiet time," "relaxation," and "head ed." Or you might call the activities "centering."

8. *Should we hold a discussion after each activity?*

It's up to you. Our strong advice is not to program a discussion so that a "lesson" is learned from these activities. If a discussion happens, beautiful. If not, that's all right too, because these activities may affect areas of ourselves that are not easily discussed.

9. *Can the activities be used to work with specific problems, such as test anxiety and poor self-image?*

There is substantial evidence that centering techniques, particularly imagery, can be very useful in both of these areas. For example, it has been shown that imagining taking a test can reduce anxiety and increase scores in an actual test situation. Some teachers have found it helpful to have all of their students imagine performing an activity that may cause anxiety, such as taking a test or making a speech. Because relaxation is the opposite of anxiety, all of the mental and physical relaxation exercises in this book can be helpful. In addition, having children focus on taking deep, smooth breaths has been found to decrease anxiety.

Self-image is one of those vague terms that's difficult to define; however, one way to do so is to think of it as an image of the self (you) performing some activity. For example, a poor sports self-image might be an image, perhaps a memory, of yourself performing incompetently at some sport. Creative teachers have devised imagination games in which children imagined themselves enjoying various aspects of sports: the feeling of stretching their bodies, the smell of the air outdoors, the movement of a ball through space. Games such as this make the point that enjoyment, not competence, is the most important goal of sports. Nevertheless, imagination games have also been used successfully to increase competence in basketball, skiing, and other sports. Also, imagination games can be devised to improve self-image in social skills, academic performance, and other areas of concern to students.

10. *Inasmuch as these are innovative techniques, will I encounter any trouble from administrators when I use these activities in the classroom?*

Probably not, but you should be prepared to articulate some good reasons for using them. You should be ready to explain that these techniques help children learn better by promoting relaxed alertness, and that they build positive self-image and enhance creativity. It is also important to mention that children find these activities interesting and relevant. If you think your administrator might object to any of the activities, have him read this book. Most administrators who do so tend to become excited by the possibilities it represents.

Sources

GENERAL

GOLAS, T. *The Lazy Man's Guide to Enlightenment*. Palo Alto, Calif.: The Seed Center, 1972.

GOVINDA, L. *Way of the White Cloud*. Berkeley, Calif.: Shambala Publications, 1971.

HOLT, J. *Escape from Childhood*. New York: Dutton, 1974.

HUXLEY, A. *Island*. New York: Harper & Row, 1972.

Journal of Transpersonal Psychology.

KRISHNAMURTI, J. *Education and the Significance of Life*. New York: Harper & Row, 1953.

ORNSTEIN, R. *The Psychology of Consciousness*. San Francisco: W. H. Freeman, 1972.

PEARCE, J. *The Crack in the Cosmic Egg*. New York: Simon and Schuster, Pocket Books, 1973.

PIAGET, J. *The Construction of Reality in the Child*. New York: Ballantine, 1954.

REPS, P. *Be! New Uses for the Human Instrument.* New York: Weatherhill, 1971.

RICHARDS, M. C. *Centering.* Middletown, Conn.: Wesleyan University Press, 1969.

RELAXATION

GUNTHER, B. *Sense Relaxation.* New York: Macmillan, Collier Books, 1968.

JACOBSON, E. O. *You Must Relax.* New York: McGraw-Hill, 1957.

————. *Anxiety and Tension Control.* Philadelphia: Lippincott, 1964.

SCHULTZ, J. H., and LUTHE, W. *Autogenic Training: A Psychophysiological Approach to Psychotherapy.* New York: Grune & Stratton, 1959.

STRETCHING, YOGA, BODY AWARENESS

BARLOW, W. "Psychosomatic Problems in Postural Re-education." *The Lancet,* September 24, 1955, 659–64.

DOWNING, G. *The Massage Book.* Berkeley, Calif.: Bookworks (distributed by Random House), 1972.

FELDENKRAIS, M. *Awareness Through Movement.* New York: Harper & Row, 1972.

IYENGAR, B. K. S. *Light on Yoga.* New York: Schocken Books, 1966.

KELEMAN, S. *Bio-Energetic Concepts of Grounding.* San Francisco: Lodestar Press, 1970.

LAGERWERFF, E. B., and PERLROTH, K. A. *Mensendieck: Your Posture and Your Pain.* New York: Doubleday, Anchor Books, 1973.

LOWEN, A. *The Betrayal of the Body.* New York: Macmillan, 1967.

LUCE, G. G. *Body Time.* New York: Pantheon, 1971.

ROLF, I. P. "Structural Integration." *Journal of the Institute for the Comparative Study of History, Philosophy and the Sciences.* 1, no. 1 (June, 1963).

DREAMS

DOWNING, J. *Dreams and Nightmares.* New York: Harper & Row, 1973.

FARADAY, A. *Dream Power.* New York: Coward, McCann & Geoghegan, 1972.

NOONE, R. *In Search of the Dream People.* New York: Morrow, 1972.

MOVEMENT

FELDENKRAIS, M. *Body and Mature Behavior.* New York: International Universities Press, 1970.

FENG, G., and WILKERSON, H. *Tai-Chi: A Way of Centering and I Ching.* New York: Macmillan, Collier Books, 1969.

HUANG, A. *Embrace Tiger, Return to Mountain.* Moab, Utah: Real People Press, 1973.

SPOLIN, V. *Improvisations for the Theatre.* Evanston, Ill.: Northwestern University Press, 1963.

MEDITATION

CHANG, C. *The Practice of Zen.* London: Rider, 1959.

EVANS-WENTZ, W. *Tibetan Yoga and Secret Doctrines.* New York: Oxford University Press, 1935.

FENG, G., and WILKERSON, H. *Tai-Chi: A Way of Centering and I Ching.* New York: Macmillan, Collier Books, 1969.

KENNETT, J. *Selling Water by the River.* New York: Random House, Vintage Books, 1972.

LUK, C. *The Secrets of Chinese Meditation.* London: Rider, 1964.

NARANJO, C., and ORNSTEIN, R. *On the Psychology of Meditation.* New York: Viking, 1971.

TRUNGPA, C. *Meditation in Action.* Berkeley, Calif.: Shambala Publications, 1969.

IMAGERY

AHSEN, A. *Eidetic Behavior.* Yonkers, N.Y.: Eidetic Publishing House, 1973.

———. *Basic Concepts in Eidetic Psychotherapy.* New York: Branden House, 1973.

MASTERS, R., and HOUSTON, J. *Mind Games.* New York: Viking, 1972.

SINGER, J. *Daydreaming.* New York: Random House, 1966.

WOLPE, J., and LAZARUS, A. *Behavior Therapy Techniques.* Long Island City, N.Y.: Pergamon Press, 1966.

HEALTH

SAMUELS, M., and BENNETT, H. *The Well Body Book.* New York: Random House, 1973.

SOBEL, D., and HORNBACHER, F. *An Everyday Guide to Your Health.* New York: Grossman Publishers, 1973.

STORYTELLING

Shah, I. *Caravan of Dreams.* London: Octagon Press, 1968(a).

SHAH, I. *The Pleasantries of the Incredible Mulla Nasrudin.* London: Jonathan Cape, 1968(b).

SHAH, I. *The Dermis Probe.* London: Jonathan Cape, 1970.

☐ Please charge my ☐ MasterCard ☐ Visa

Credit Card # _____ Exp. date _____

Signature _____

☐ Enclosed is my check or money order.
  *Publisher pays postage and handling charges
  for prepaid and charge card orders.

☐ Bill me.

Name _____ Apt. # _____

Address _____

City/State _____ Zip _____

MERCHANDISE TOTAL		
ADD:	SALES TAX FOR YOUR STATE	
	*12% POSTAGE AND HANDLING	
TOTAL: CHECK ENCLOSED		

PLEASE ALLOW FOUR WEEKS FOR DELIVERY

Send your order to:
Prentice Hall Press Mail Order Billing
Route 59 at Brook Hill Drive
West Nyack, NY 10994

Phone (201) 767-5937 for
any additional ordering
information.